Out of the Deep

Out of the Deep

Prayer as Protest

GORDON MURSELL

Foreword by David Sheppard

Darton Longman and Todd
London

First published in 1989 by
Darton Longman & Todd Ltd
89 Lillie Road, London SW6 1UD

British Library Cataloguing in Publication Data

Mursell, Gordon
  Out of the deep.
  1. Christian life. Prayer
  I. Title
  248.3'2

  ISBN 0–232–51844–0

Typeset by Input Typesetting Ltd
London SW19 8DR
Printed in Great Britain by
Courier International Ltd, Tiptree, Essex

To the memory of
Basil Fletcher-Jones
priest, teacher and friend

Contents

Foreword *by David Sheppard*   ix

Acknowledgements   xi

Note   xii

Introduction   1

1   The Cloud-Covered Mountain
From the Book of Exodus to Golgotha   12

2   The Garden of Delights
The Song of Songs   26

3   The Waters of the Deep
The Psalms and the Book of Job   42

4   The Burning Fiery Furnace
Spirituality and the Apocalypse   62

5   The Call of the Wilderness
The Desert Tradition   79

6   The Child's Question
Julian of Norwich   91

7   The Interior Protest
St Teresa of Avila   102

8   The Pilgrim's Protest
John Bunyan   118

9   The Land of Lost Content
The Poets of the First World War   135

10   The Songs of Freedom
The Holocaust and Beyond   160

Index   175

Foreword

Gordon Mursell has given us a book on spirituality to be recommended to every kind of Christian. It is a book for all seasons, to be savoured piecemeal, a chapter at a time: it will be a treat for those who take it away for a quiet day or on retreat to reflect on. And it will beckon us back later for recall, action and further study. He has digested profound learning and leads us into its fruits in engaging ways.

It is catholic in the widest sense, drawing on the experience of men and women of God from within the pages of scripture and without, embracing Catholic and Evangelical, Contemplative and Activist, Conformist and Dissenter alike.

Still more, it is anchored in experience, drawing deeply from his own wells, past and present – being made foolish through failure in sport at school, facing as a teenager the death of his father, recognizing his feelings on visiting an old lady in a shack in Namibia.

The prayer of protest he writes about is more than the painful expression of personal or corporate experience, more than a cry to God to hear and respond.

It is also a challenge to belief. And it will help many in their believing who cannot stomach snappy catch answers which avoid our deep questions.

It is a personal delight to be made aware in these pages of his continuing journey of discipleship since I ordained Gordon Mursell in Liverpool. I have followed with admiration the way he has gone on using the raw material of his experience in Liverpool, South East London and in teaching students as a disciple of Christ. He shows how God's wisdom of the centuries stands in the world of urban and modern realities.

Out of the Deep is a profoundly wordly book, affirming, challenging and setting out to change the world in which we live. It is also heavenly, because it is ultimately about a world yet to come, where God is and justice is. It accepts and faces the reality of the world of now; here and now it offers not just a general hope of God's justice, but also personal glimpses of God's presence. I hope that many will enter on this spiritual pilgrimage with Gordon Mursell.

+David Liverpool

Acknowledgements

I owe a great debt to my friends and colleagues at Salisbury and Wells Theological College for an immense amount of advice and encouragement in writing this book; among them Dr Trevor Dennis for extensive help with Chapter 1; Stephen Barton, now Lecturer in New Testament at Durham University, whose wisdom and guidance helped me in the preparation of Chapter 4; Judith Maltby for much wise advice with Chapter 8; and Nicholas Bradbury for advice and constant support over too many years to mention. I am also very grateful to a small group of students at the college whose enthusiasm and interest helped me greatly with Chapter 9.

I owe a great deal to Sister Benedicta Ward SLG for taking the time to read drafts of many of the chapters, and for much help and guidance with them; to David Meara for much help with Chapter 9 in particular; and to Canon David Jennings for helping me with ideas for the last chapter.

I am enormously grateful to Lesley Riddle, not only for encouraging me to write in the first place but for unfailing help and support from start to finish.

Finally I owe my greatest debt of gratitude to Professor Leslie Houlden, who has given me far more of his wisdom and critical advice, not to mention friendship, than expected or deserved. I am certainly not the first, and will equally certainly not be the last, among Anglican writers and clergy to be aware of how much I owe him.

To the people of St Mary's, Walton, Liverpool, and of St John's, East Dulwich, among whom I lived and worked for thirteen years and from whom almost all the inspiration for this book came, I cannot begin to be grateful enough.

Gordon Mursell

Note

Introduction

When I was sixteen my father died. I remember the day vividly. I was at school on a bright September morning. One of the teachers appeared in my classroom and beckoned to me. When I followed him to his room I was mildly surprised to see that my brother, who was two years younger than me, was there as well. As soon as we were seated the teacher told us that our father had had a coronary thrombosis and had died more or less instantaneously. Those who have experienced the shock of sudden bereavement will know the surge of unreality, the host of ludicrously trivial thoughts which rise from nowhere while the mind struggles to adjust to the new reality. I remember wth appalling clarity that my first thought on hearing the news had to do with the extraordinarily chaotic state of the teacher's collar and tie. The second thought, as my brother and I emerged from the teacher's room, was of the imminent thrill about to be afforded us by being driven home in my uncle's large and grand car. Grief, the awareness of what we had lost, the shock and incredulity and anger: none of these things impinged nearly as much at that moment as the sudden unexpected sense of deliverance from a morning of mathematics and French.

Later, of course, they did, in many and various ways, of which the strangest took place over a year later when I assumed I had got over the tragedy completely, as any grown-up person should. (It was later still before I discovered that bereavement was not something you 'get over', like mumps, but something you spend your life trying to come to terms with and often not succeeding.) I was in Rome for some months studying music before going to university. I had not hitherto thought very much about God in my life; indeed I had rejected the more or less standard confirmation classes which most of my peers attended. In Rome, however, God (or at least the rumour of him) was unavoidable: even the public lavatories had crucifixes, and I remember watching with a kind of horrified fascination as pious Romans seeking to knock a few years off their time in Purgatory grunted and sweated their way up the Scala Santa near the Lateran basilica while a grizzled and cassocked priest sold trinkets in a box-office by the door. I was not impressed.

I was impressed, however, albeit reluctantly, by the immense basilica of St Paul Outside-the-Walls which stands alone opposite a park in a dowdy suburb. When I went there on a cold December afternoon, teenagers were playing football in the park, and hurtling round the piazza on motor scooters. I was suddenly gripped by a terrible loneliness; and when I entered the vast and dimly-lit basilica with its eighty marble columns and gorgeous mosaics I was overwhelmed, not just with awe but with anger, at the God who had taken away my father and yet seemed to enjoy dwelling in buildings of such icy magnificence: anger too at a world which could go happily about its business as heedless of my loss as God was. I gave vent to my feelings in tears of fury and self-pity; and neither the laughing footballers nor the God of the great basilica took any notice. Yet I was left with a strangely clear awareness that it was *all right* to be angry and lonely and to say so – and that, in some wholly inexplicable sense, what I had said had been heard.

That kind of prayer, with its strange mix of doubt, anger and puzzlement, is the subject of this book. I have called it, for want of a better description, the prayer of protest. You will not find much about this in manuals of spirituality, though some books in which the subject is addressed are listed at the end of this chapter. Yet for millions of people it is the first (and sometimes the only) kind of prayer that is ever experienced. It might reasonably be dismissed as wishful thinking – our deep need to believe in a God eventually convincing us that there is one. Or it might be regarded as a very primitive, almost animal form of prayer, rapidly left behind by expert practitioners of the art on their way to the heights of contemplative ecstasy. What caused me to consider writing this was the persistent conviction, born of my own experience, that this kind of praying was neither as phoney nor as infantile as might first be supposed; and what caused me actually to write it was the discovery that many before me had thought so too.

The word 'protest' today often carries overtones of radical political action, of demonstrations or even insurrections against the secular power. Yet protest, in its simplest and primal form, is integral to the natural instincts of all creatures. In his classic study *Attachment and Loss*, John Bowlby distinguishes three stages in the process that occurs when a child is separated from its mother: protest, despair, and finally detachment.[1] The protest stage may last for anything from a few hours to a week or more; and during it the child will seek to recapture its mother 'by the full exercise of his limited resources'. It is a period usually marked by furious activity and the expression of unfettered emotion; and the more isolated the child, the more vigorous the protest.[2]

The word 'protest' does not, however, simply imply an act of dissent or disapproval. It derives from the Latin verb *protestor*, which means 'to bear solemn witness' or to declare something formally and in public, as when someone protests his innocence: other English words, such as 'testify' or 'testimony', come from the same root. The word has then a twofold meaning: it describes both the act of questioning or dissenting *from* something and the act of bearing witness *to* something. This dual significance is exemplified in the religious term 'Protestant', meaning someone who both dissents from Roman Catholicism and 'bears witness' to a different and distinctive set of beliefs. It is an action that is at once negative and positive, but never passive: it is always something you do or express, not something that is simply done to you. It is in both its meanings an integral part of human (indeed of creaturely) behaviour; and underlying it is our common need to make sense of our world and our experience and to discern some kind of meaning and order within them. When that meaning and order are disturbed we protest; and our protest is both a challenge to the disturber and an honest laying-bare of how we feel. Of itself it is morally neutral, as susceptible of misuse as any other aspect of human behaviour; but properly used it is an indispensable dimension of our growth towards maturity.

Yet even if protest can be seen as an integral part of human experience, can the same be said of prayer? One recent writer refers to a therapist who believed that those who prayed did so because they could not face reality;[3] and it is true that some manuals of instruction about prayer create the unmistakable impression that prayer has very little to do with the 'real' world of most people's experience. The point is sometimes made the other way round: Martin Luther King once wrote: 'A man said to me, "I believe in integration, but I know it will not come until God wants it to come. You Negroes should stop protesting and start praying." '[4] Either way protest and prayer might appear to be activities entirely independent of one another. But life and prayer often appear to be like that; and perhaps one of the reasons why people so rarely have recourse to prayer is precisely because it seems to bear so little relation to anything else they do. And yet the fact remains that one of the few moments at which people are still apt to pray, almost regardless of their religious beliefs, is at those crisis points which drive us to protest. On 8 December 1988 a London newspaper carried a photograph of Keya, an eighteen-year-old woman whose son had drowned in a flood disaster in Bangladesh. Beneath the picture was a report in which Keya described what had happened. First there was heavy rain followed by strong winds, and then a tidal wave: 'We were praying. The wind started blowing stronger. My husband came and held me tightly. At the same time I felt a hot air with tremendous speed take away our roof. I cried in fear and asked God for mercy. We heard people screaming and children crying.'[5] Their adobe house was destroyed and their barn with all their grain swept away: their livestock was killed and their crops ruined. God did not, it seems, answer Keya's prayer, or at any rate not in the way she doubtless wanted. But that did not stop her praying. It could well be argued that such prayer is no more than an instinctive response to a violent disturbance of life's normal pattern; and it certainly

4

needs to be emphasized that protest of this kind, understood both as a complaint, a cry for help, and as an articulation of what you are feeling, is still intrinsically therapeutic, whether or not there is a God who listens.

But what if there is? Is it right or fair, or even appropriate, to cry out to him in protest? Should we not rather look to him for assistance in coming to terms with what has happened, not for an escape route to avoid it, let alone an outright supervention to prevent it? Or should we regard him simply as a convenient sounding-board to whom we can express our feelings without any expectation of a response? Our answers to these questions will depend partly on what kind of a God we believe in; and we will reflect a little more on the relationship between belief and prayer in Chapter 1. But they will also depend on what we understand prayer to be.

For if, as Christians believe, prayer is the language of a relationship, then there is surely something odd about the fact that the language in which it is customarily expressed often bears very little resemblance to the language we now use in other relationships. It is true that, however we understand God, our relationship with him is not going to be the same as those we have with other human beings: indeed in some respects it does not even resemble anything analogous to human experience. Yet human analogies, in the end, are all we have to go on; and if, as Christians also believe, the primary characteristic of God is love, then our human relationships with those we love are surely going to provide us with guidelines for our relationship with God. And if this is so, certain things follow.

First, prayer will not just be an occasional expression of delight or respect. It will be hard work, requiring perseverance and effort and unrelenting honesty. Secondly the agenda for prayer will embrace the whole of our lives, not only (or even primarily) the religious parts. If our prayer is no more than the spiritual equivalent of talking about the weather it is perhaps not surprising that it fails to satisfy, let alone to attract. But if, as with any intimate human relationship, nothing is too important or too trivial to be excluded, then our feelings, our questions, our cries for help – in short our protests – will have a place within it. It is the central assumption of this book, as of each of the characters whose ideas are explored, that our relationship with God is a two-way process involving not just reverence but challenge, not just passivity but protest. For the more you love someone, the more of yourself you will want to share with them; and the more you share with them, the more your love for one another will grow.

That is not to say that all prayer is to be understood as protest, even in the broad and twofold sense in which protest is defined here. Any relationship that consisted exclusively of one person screaming at, or crying to, the other would wither from lack of the reciprocity that is its oxygen. But by the same token any relationship whose principal ingredient consisted of formal acts of prepared and structured conversation, presupposing extensive preliminary practice and skill and a considerable capacity for literary eloquence, would surely be seriously deficient in the freedom and spontaneity we take for granted elsewhere. The argument is not that protest is the only, or even the primary, ingredient of prayer, but that it belongs, together wth contemplation, intercession, penance and so on, as a vital and distinctive part of the whole.

The prayer of protest then, is the expression before God of our anxieties, our experiences of injustice and suffering, our feelings of outrage or despair or anger, and our needs and hopes for the future. Such expression may not always be very articulate: it may not even require words. Gandhi once wrote: 'Prayer is not asking. It is a longing of the soul. It is daily admission of one's weakness . . . It is better in prayer to have a heart without words than words without a heart.'[6] More importantly it may or may not expect an answer; but its effectiveness and value do not depend simply on whether an answer is received. There is an excellent illustration of this point near the beginning of Elie Wiesel's terrifying autobiographical book *Night*, when the young Elie asks Moche the Beadle, his Jewish religious instructor, why he prays:

> He explained to me with great insistence that every question possessed a power that did not lie in the answer.

'Man raises himself toward God by the questions he asks Him,' he was fond of repeating. 'That is the true dialogue. Man questions God and God answers. But we don't understand His answers. We can't understand them. Because they come from the depth of the soul, and they stay there until death. You will find the true answers, Eliezer, only within yourself!'

'And why do you pray, Moche?' I asked him.

'I pray to the God within me that He will give me the strength to ask Him the right questions.'[7]

This is not of course to say that when we pray we do not want answers; but it is to suggest that the prayer of protest can and does have value irrespective of whether any answer, let alone the one we long for, is received. We will explore in Chapter 3 how the Psalms, which remain the classic exemplars of the prayer of protest, reflect the integrity and the therapeutic value of thus articulating your experience: indeed each of the writers or themes considered underlines the crucial point that the honest laying bare of your feelings and questions is essential if you are ever to move on beyond them. If that were true in any age of human history, it is perhaps particularly relevant to this one; and some of the ways in which it has been addressed in the twentieth century will be explored in the final two chapters. But it is also part of our purpose to underline the extent to which it has remained a common theme of, and challenge to, spirituality from the earliest times. We make no claim to comprehensive treatment of the subject but merely seek to illustrate it by reference to a variety of individuals and groups who have engaged with it.

Protest against suffering (especially undeserved suffering) recurs in many of the following chapters, as might be expected: no other subject has had so constant and significant an influence on the prayer of protest. In Chapter 1 the spirituality of Moses and Jeremiah leads us to the prayer of Jesus at Gethsemane and Golgotha: his cries of protest at what happens to him, and the terrible silence which greets them, form the *locus classicus* and the constant reference point for those who follow. In Chapter 2, which explores the spirituality of the Song of Songs, the focus shifts to the nature of love as letting go, and the extent to which suffering and even death can be seen as integral dimensions of it. In Chapter 3 we consider some of the vast range of experiences which are addressed by the Psalms and the Book of Job, and their abiding relevance to our situation today. Chapter 4 explores a different aspect: the spirituality of apocalyptic, and those whose furious and courageous protest against injustice and suffering speaks both to our understanding of prayer and to our picture of God. Chapter 5, on desert spirituality, returns in a new context to a theme that appears in Chapter 1: the desert, like Golgotha, is a place where our prayer of protest and God's intersect; and from the book of Hosea to Charles de Foucauld our outcry at a Creator who appears to sit idly by while his creatures suffer collides with God's plea to his people to repent of their shortsighted self-seeking before it is too late. Julian of Norwich, who forms the subject of Chapter 6, helps us further to see how closely childlike love and protest are connected; and in Julian's understanding of 'beholding' the apparently disjunct experiences of contemplation and protest come together. St Teresa's (Chapter 7) and John Bunyan's (Chapter 8) protests to God in the face of their own suffering offer new insights from very different contexts; and in Chapter 9 the subject receives its most searching exploration in the poetry of the First World War. In the concluding Chapter 10 the relevance of all this to our own situation is examined: it is because we live in a world whose catastrophes are significantly more predictable and avoidable than hitherto, and which are frequently the consequence not only of evil people behaving wickedly, but of good people remaining silent, that this subject continues to demand our attention today.

Yet protest is not the only aspect of our study. The nature of play, and the use of the imagination in prayer; the experience of doubt; the spirituality of hope; the discovery of God in the midst of the everyday, and the connection between intimate love and the prayer of protest: these and other crucial dimensions of our subject appear at various points along our way. These utterly diverse themes, and the people and movements who articulate them, have been chosen not because they are the only representatives of the prayer of protest, but because from different perspectives they share a concern with one underlying theme: the perennial and perplexing capacity of human beings to wrestle with, and try to make sense of, their experience of life in the light of their relationship with God. For some, that relationship will be one of the deepest intimacy – though, even for them, it will never become a cosy or introverted affair: for others it will be a relationship riddled with doubt and ambivalence and yawning uncertainty about whether it even exists. For all of them the terrible experience of no longer being in control of one's life prompts the decision not simply to stay meekly silent, but to protest – to challenge, to question and to bear witness to what you are experiencing. If you have ever, at any time or for any reason, shared something of that experience, or known and loved others who have, then this book may speak to you.

If it does, you may find, as Sheila Cassidy has put it, that the more you pray, the more you will want to;[8] and that the more you come to be able to express and articulate your own experience the more likely you are to find a way through it. Throughout western spirituality, from the Book of Exodus to Martin Luther King and Elie Wiesel, protest – understood in the twofold sense of challenge and bearing witness – has remained a constant feature: alongside the timeless power of formal liturgy or the distant reaches of contemplative intimacy, the prayer of protest has held its place, restoring the prophetic and the charismatic, and above all the primary role of prayer as helping people to respond to, and make sense of, what was happening to them, whenever such themes were in danger of being swamped in a lather of bland or tired institutional froth. The concern of this book is not to introduce the subject, as though it were a novelty or gimmick, but to draw attention to what has always been there.

Two final points remain. First this is not primarily about political or social protest: the central concern is not protest aganst the world, but protest against God. Inevitably, however, the two frequently become one; and some people who appear are concerned equally with both. This is emphatically as it should be: far too much spirituality suffers from being divorced from the social or the political when it should be equipping us to address them. Dorothée Soelle expresses this vividly:

> The God of the Bible is the deepest regression we need, and at the same time he is the process of increasing justice. He stands for letting oneself go *and* exerting oneself, for the opened hand *and* the clenched fist. The goal of all religions is to reach this farthest point, to experience the deepest self-confirmation and yet to return, and to communicate the experience that we are a part of the whole. The false division of labour that specializes and polarizes into prayers and battlers is thus at an end, and we learn that our hands have a double use: to pray *and* to do battle.[9]

There are, however, many books whose central focus is political spirituality or protest against the world: this book, whose focus is protest against God, is written to complement them, while recognizing that the two can never be entirely separated. But it is also written to emphasize the fact that the prayer of protest, far from being the creation of liberation thelogians, has been central to Jewish and Christian spirituality from the beginning. To say this is not to criticize liberation theology: on the contrary, it is to underline its importance.

Finally all that has been written so far may create the impression that the prayer of protest is an unequivocally gloomy affair concerned exclusively with suffering and death. In fact the opposite is the case: it is precisely *because* it is concerned to confront these things that it is also concerned to go on beyond them. It is because Judaism and Christianity treat evil with the utmost seriousness that they are able to treat playfulness and joy with the utmost reverence. Each chapter draws attention to an apparent paradox: that the prayer of protest and challenge is closely related to the experience of intimacy and mutual love. But the paradox is more apparent than real: from the psalmist to John Bunyan, from

Moses to Wilfred Owen, the characters whose spirituality we explore had discovered what most children know better than we do: that our honest and blundering attempts to express how we feel not only liberate us from the stifling stereotypes in which we are confined. They also expose our urgent need for acceptance, affirmation and unconditional love and, by so doing, lead us and lay us open to its infinite source.

NOTES

1 See John Bowlby, *Attachment and Loss*, vol. II, *Separation* (London, Penguin, 1975), p. 47.
2 Bowlby, op. cit. vol. I, *Attachment* (London, Penguin, 1971), p. 51.
3 Jack Babuscio, *We Speak for Ourselves*, 2nd edn (London, SPCK, 1988), p. 11.
4 From 'The answer to a perplexing question' in *Strength to Love* (London, Collins Fontana, 1963), p. 131.
5 *The Independent*, 8 December 1988.
6 *Selected Writings of Mahatma Gandhi*, ed. Ronald Duncan (London, Collins Fontana, 1971), p. 273.
7 Elie Wiesel, *Night*, tr. Rodway (London, Penguin, 1981), pp. 14–15.
8 Sheila Cassidy, *Sharing the Darkness* (London, DLT, 1988), pp. 141–2.
9 Dorothée Soelle, *The Inward Road* (London, DLT, 1979), p. 69.

FURTHER READING

Friedrich Heiler, *Prayer: history and psychology*, tr. McComb (New York, Oxford University Press, 1958), esp. ch. IX.
Ann and Barry Ulanov, *Primary Speech: a psychology of prayer*. London, SCM, 1985.
Gonville ffrench-Beytagh, *A Glimpse of Glory* (London, DLT, 1986), esp. Part I.

1

The Cloud-Covered Mountain
From the Book of Exodus to Golgotha

The way we address particular people depends, more often than not, on the way we think about them: ceremonial obeisance would be as inappropriate in the playground or post office as backslapping jollity on a first encounter with the Pope. The same is true of the way we pray; and reflection on the subject will be of limited value unless some account is taken of how the person praying views the object or recipient of the prayer. In the case of the ancient Israelites, with whom our exploration begins, that object or person was the one God Yahweh, who they believed to have created the cosmos and everything in it and might therefore be thought to be worthy of the utmost reverence. But their view of God was shot through with paradox. On the one hand he was infinitely and dangerously holy, transcendent and omnipotent: on the other he was in effect a marriage-partner, because he had made a solemn and mutually binding covenant with the people he had chosen, a covenant whose nature and character were expressed as often in the language of intimate love as in that of hushed awe. If that sounds to us like the lowest kind of patriarchalism, it is all the more important to emphasize that for the Israelites it was the highest kind of divinity, making accessible a God who was both intimate enough to hear their prayers and strong enough to respond: a God great enough to hold the universe in thrall, yet small enough to care about (and even be swayed by) its most fragile creatures.

It is within the context of that God, and above all of that covenant, that the 'prayer of protest' as it appears in the Bible needs to be seen. It was because the Israelites believed they had experienced God's love that they felt able to cry out, or question or challenge, or simply run to him, when things went wrong; and even when they were able to see that what had happened might not be his fault, they never ceased to believe that it was his concern. Their relationship with God was a two-way process, involving not just reverence but challenge, not just passivity but protest, whatever the cost and risk involved.

That is not to say that the Hebrew picture of God remained static from one end of the Bible to the other; but it is to say that that picture almost always presupposed a God who was, so to speak, on their side, and to whom they therefore had a right to look both for an explanation and for solace and company when something went wrong. It is also to emphasize the influence this had on their understanding and experience of prayer. For the way we picture God does profoundly affect the way we pray. If God is only an absolute monarch, in unrestricted control of all that is and will be, then prayer will always be couched in the language of the courtier, manoeuvring and grovelling by turns, anxiously placating and insistently praising the embodiment of unbridled omnipotence. Moreover it will be both inappropriate and even dangerous to approach such a God directly: so prayer has to become the discourse of the professional guru, a kind of secret and scented code known only to the inner élite, by which the people are kept happy and God kept safely at a distance. If God is a lifeless idol or national mascot, prayer is likely to be reduced to the empty ritual posturings of the religious hireling, with his finger in the wind and his eye on the Prime Minister. But if God is a parent or a friend, or even (as in some of the Old Testament writings) a lover, then the agenda for prayer will encompass the whole of human experience and its language will be neither that of a court nor that of a social convention, nor even that of a church, but of an intimate and loving relationship. This is not to imply that the biblical writers saw the relationship as being one of equality: indeed even at his most tender God was always the Holy One, mysterious and set apart and sometimes capable of dangerous anger. What it does imply is that nothing was too secular or too painful to be shared with him, and that even when her

13

behaviour was most blatantly unworthy or sinful Israel never lost her right to be heard.

Some of the implications of this approach can be seen in one of the finest Old Testament illustrations of the prayer of protest: the story of the golden calf (Exod. 32). Moses, whom God has called to lead his people out of enslavement in Egypt, brings them into the wilderness and to the foot of Mount Sinai. It is there that God gives them the twin foundations of Israelite life and spirituality: the Law and the covenant, the former the indispensable guide to life and holiness, and the latter the unique and intimate relationship with God to which Israel is called. Like the man and the woman in Eden, however, the people become impatient and distrustful, unable to resist the temptation to replace this puzzlingly personal God with a substitute they can challenge and control.

The story is a narrative masterpiece, and is told on two levels. On the higher level, in more senses than one, is Moses, who has ascended Mount Sinai alone in order to receive from God the tablets on which the Law was inscribed. Cloud covers the mountain, and 'to the watching Israelites, the glory of Yahweh looked like a devouring fire on the mountain top' (Exod. 24:17). After six days of waiting, God calls Moses from within the cloud; and Moses enters the cloud to be alone with God for the symbolic period of forty days and nights (Exod. 24:18). Yet here, as so often in the Bible, this intimacy with God is no cosy act of contemplation designed to cosset one individual's ego, but an encounter concerned entirely with the relationship between God and his people. True spirituality is never the pursuit of private perfection, never a purely interior affair: the search in the cloudy darkness for an encounter with God will be fruitless if it is not overridingly concerned with the whole life of the people outside.

On the lower level, at the mountain's foot, are the people of Israel, waiting patiently for Moses to return. After a while, they become impatient:

When the people saw that Moses was a long time before coming down the mountain, they gathered round Aaron and said to him, 'Get to work, make us a god to go at our head; for that Moses, the man who brought us here from Egypt – we do not know what has become of him.' (Exod. 32:1–2)

Aaron obligingly complies, and under his direction the people create the golden calf. Unwilling to wait upon God's will, they yield to temptation: they create their own god, an idol who would do whatever they wanted. It is a recurrent temptation: Christians have often preferred false gods who will canonize their party politics, bless their armies or (most subtle of all) legitimate their own private religious beliefs, rather than the real God who might challenge them. The golden calf is a symbol of our dogged persistence in searching for a mascot instead of a saviour, a lifeless idol instead of a living God.

But the real point of the story consists in the contrast it offers between two kinds of protest. The people of Israel protest against God; but instead of challenging him directly they simply persuade Aaron to help them create a more malleable substitute. When Aaron is later confronted by the angry Moses he puts all the blame on the people and offers a feeble and blatantly untrue explanation of what happened:

> Aaron replied, 'My lord should not be so angry. You yourself know what a bad state these people are in! They said to me, "Make us a god to go at our head; for that Moses, the man who brought us here from Egypt – we do not know what has become of him." I then said to them, "Anyone with gold, strip it off!" They gave it to me. I threw it into the fire and out came this calf!' (Exod. 32:22–24)

On the mountain summit, however, God tells Moses what is happening and declares his intention of destroying his reprobate people:

> Yahweh then said to Moses, 'Go down at once, for your people whom you brought here from Egypt have become corrupt . . . I know these people; I know how obstinate

15

they are! So leave me now, so that my anger can blaze at them and I can put an end to them! I shall make a great nation out of you instead.' (Exod. 32:7, 9–10)

But Moses will not leave him. Far from basking in his new-found destiny he does the opposite. Alone before God, he protests on behalf of his people:

Moses tried to pacify Yahweh his God. 'Yahweh,' he said, 'why should your anger blaze at your people, whom you have brought out of Egypt by your great power and mighty hand? Why should the Egyptians say, "He brought them out with evil intention, to slaughter them in the mountains and wipe them off the face of the earth"? Give up your burning wrath; relent over this disaster intended for your people. Remember your servants Abraham, Isaac and Jacob, to whom you swore by your very self and made this promise: "I shall make your offspring as numerous as the stars of heaven . . ."' ' Yahweh then relented over the disaster which he had intended to inflict on his people. (Exod. 32:11–14)

Moses both challenges God and corrects him: when God tells him that *his* people are misbehaving Moses responds by pointing out that they are *God's* people, not his. Later Moses prays to God to forgive his people, offering his own life as an expiation of their sin (Exod. 32:30–33). The relationship between God and Moses is one of extraordinary intimacy: God speaks to him 'face to face, as a man talks to his friend' (Exod. 33:11). Moses, it appears, comes as close as is humanly possible to a face-to-face encounter with God, though it is important to note that such encounters can only be received as a gift, never deserved or earned; and when Moses actually asks for one (Exod. 33:18), he only sees God's back.[1] The contrast between Aaron and Moses is instructive: Aaron, seduced by dreams of easy and instant success, is in the end too weak even to restrain the people: Moses, alone on the mountain, is strong enough to restrain God.

Yet the story of the golden calf is not a tale about a single heroic figure, storming Olympus with herculean power; nor is it simply a description of someone reminiscent of an oriental vizier, wheedling and fawning upon his master like a cat with its eye on the cream. Moses' relationship with God embodies and articulates the essence of the prayer of protest: it is characterized by conversation, argument and challenge. He protests, both in the sense of bearing witness to the truth of the situation and in the sense of calling upon God to change his mind. He uses his relationship with God for the good of others; and his experience on the cloud-covered mountain combines patent attentiveness with active and costly inter-cession. He refuses to leave God or let go of him, even when commanded to do so (Exod. 32:10), with the result that he and God together determine the outcome. At the foot of the mountain there is clamour and feasting, noise and ritual dances; at the top there is a hidden wrestling-match in the darkness. Yet it is precisely there that the matter is ultimately decided; and the story ends with God not only relenting over his plans for punishment but also renewing his intimate covenant relationship with the people he loves too much to destroy.

You could by this time be forgiven for wondering what all this has to do with us today, in a world where nuclear power and AIDS and the destruction of the environment pose far greater threats than the manufacture of golden calves. But the spirituality of biblical stories like this one is much closer to contemporary reality than it may at first appear. For it suggests that our relationship with God will be as unpredict-able, immediate and spontaneous as any of our human relationships; like them it will be concerned with the fabric of our lives as they are, with all their earthy secularity, con-flicts over status or power, and ill-considered actions. We will experience God not as some distant and changeless dispenser of fate but as friend and partner, as judge and even as adver-sary; but above all as one who speaks but never compels, who leaves us free to make our own decisions, and yet who cares so passionately about us that he can neither avoid expressing his feelings when we go wrong nor prevent himself forgiving us over and over again irrespective of our congenital capacity for impatience and forgetfulness. If prayer is genuinely to reflect our lives as they are, and to respond to the deepest needs and aspirations of those among whom we live, then it will be characterized not by escapist ego-trips but by challenge and question, by direct and honest confrontation with a God who will never be satisfied for as long as we skulk behind fig-leaves or fritter away our divinely given potential for maturity and fulfilment by bowing down to gods of gold and silver.

Within the Bible the prayer of protest receives its fullest treatment in the Psalms and the Book of Job; and these deserve exploration separately. In the prophetic books of the Old Testament the nature of biblical spirituality and the two-way relationship that undergirds it are further developed; and one striking element in particular is worth mentioning. Some of the prophets, perhaps most notably Jeremiah, become (even more than Moses) mouthpieces both of the people's protest to God and of God's protest to the people. Chapters 14–16 of the Book of Jeremiah illustrate this graphically: the fourteenth chapter begins with the prophet expressing in bleak and vivid imagery the predicament of his people at a time of national drought:

> The word of Yahweh that came to Jeremiah on the occasion of the drought.

> > 'Judah is in mourning,
> > her towns are pining,
> > sinking to the ground;
> > a cry goes up from Jerusalem.
> > The nobles send their servants for water,
> > they come to the water-tanks,
> > find no water,
> > and return with their pitchers empty.
> > Dismayed and bewildered,
> > they cover their heads.
> > Because the soil is all cracked
> > since the country has had no rain;

the farmers are dismayed,
they cover their heads.
Even the doe in the countryside
giving birth abandons her young,
for there is no grass;
the wild donkeys standing on the bare heights
gasp for air like jackals:
their eyes grow dim
for lack of pasture.' (Jer. 14:1–6)

Then Jeremiah rounds on God forcefully:

'Although our sins witness against us,
Yahweh, for your name's sake, intervene!
Yes, our acts of infidelity have been many,
we have sinned against you!
Yahweh, hope of Israel,
its Saviour in time of distress,
why are you like a stranger in this country,
like a traveller staying only for one night?
Why are you like someone bemused,
like a warrior who has no power to rescue?
And yet, Yahweh, you are among us,
we are called by your name.
Do not desert us!' (Jer. 14:7–9)

Slowly Jeremiah begins to see that the intimate relationship
between God and his people is imperilled. He makes a great
effort to challenge God and remind him that he alone is
Israel's hope. But this time, it seems, the Lord has had
enough:

Yahweh says this about this people, 'They take such pleasure in darting hither and thither, they cannot restrain their
feet! But Yahweh takes pleasure in them no longer; now
he will keep their guilt in mind and punish their sins'.
Yahweh then said to me, 'Do not intercede for this people
or their welfare. If they fast, I will not listen to their plea;
if they offer burnt offerings and cereal offerings I will not

accept them. Rather, I shall make an end of them by sword, famine and plague'. (Jer. 14:10–12)

Jeremiah, however, persists: he asks God why, if God means to destroy his people, there are prophets promising them peace (14:13). But the Lord's reply is relentlessly harsh: I did not send them, and both they and the people will perish because of their wickedness. There follows a powerful passage of lament:

> So say this word to them:
> 'May my eyes shed tears
> night and day, unceasingly,
> since the daughter of my people has sustained
>   a fearsome wound,
> a crippling injury.
> If I go into the counryside,
> there lie those killed by the sword;
> if I go into the city,
> I see people tortured with hunger;
> even prophets and priests
> roam the country at their wits' end.' (Jer. 14:17–18)

This is God protesting, weeping in sorrow and anger over his people's evil. And it forces Jeremiah to have recourse to the only weapon left in his armoury, the fundamental Israelite belief in themselves as God's children, entitled (as in our opening analogy) to his love not because they deserved it but because he was their parent. But God's terrible answer appears to abrogate the covenant he had made with Moses at Sinai:

> Yahweh said to me, 'Even if Moses and Samuel pleaded before me, I could not sympathise with this people! Drive them out of my sight; away with them! And if they ask you, "Where shall we go?" tell them this, "Yahweh says this:
>
> > Those for the plague, to the plague;
> > those for the sword, to the sword;

> those for famine, to famine;
> those for captivity, to captivity! . . ." '
> Who is there to pity you, Jerusalem,
> who to grieve for you,
> who to go out of his way
> and ask you how you are?
> 'You yourself have rejected me, Yahweh
>   declares,
> you have turned your back on me;
> so I have stretched my hand over you and
>   destroyed you.
> Tired of relenting,
> I have winnowed them with a winnow
> at the country's gates.
> They have been bereft, I have destroyed my
>   people,
> but they refuse to leave their ways . . .
> It is still day, but already her sun has set,
> she is dismayed and distracted;
> and the rest of them I shall consign to the
>   sword,
> to their enemies, Yahweh declares.' (Jer.
> 15:1–2, 5–7, 9)

Jeremiah's response to this fearful pronouncement is to turn in on himself, lamenting his own suffering and isolation (15:10–18), only to be told by God that he must persist in his uncompromising prophecies of doom and judgment because that alone can serve to bring Israel to its senses. And only then, on the very brink of the dissolution of the relationship that has bound Yahweh to his people, does God relent at last:

'Look, the days are coming, Yahweh declares, when people will no longer say, "As Yahweh lives who brought the Israelites out of Egypt!" but, "As Yahweh lives who brought the Israelites back from the land of the north and all the countries to which he had driven them." I shall

21

bring them back to the very soil I gave their ancestors.'
(Jer. 16:14–15)

This ferocious and intense dialogue brings both covenant
partners into raging confrontation in a way that may cause
twentieth-century readers to recoil with disapproval. We may
well question the usefulness, or even the possibility, of believing in (let alone praying to) a God who gets as angry as this;
and we may find something crude and incredible about a
religion which presupposes that natural catastrophes like
drought are the direct consequence both of the people's sin,
and of their God's wrath. Yet anger, here as in any intimate
relationship, is always and precisely the obverse of love: it is
because God loves his people so much that he gets so angry
with them when they become enslaved to evil – and by the
same token it is because Israel believes in and has experienced
God's love that she protests so furiously when that love deserts
her, or suddenly becomes conditional upon her good behaviour. It is crucial to see, first that the protests of both God
and Israel are valid, and that in their dramatic collision alone
can a way forward be found; and secondly that underlying
Israel's blunt equation of natural disaster with the will of
God lies a fierce and tenacious conviction that suffering of
any kind was to be struggled with, made sense of, and challenged in the light of her relationship with God.

It is the figure of the prophet himself, however, that deserves
emphasis for there is a powerful sense in which it anticipates
the third and last figure in our journey from Sinai to Golgotha.
For, even more than the tragic Jeremiah, Jesus both embodies
and articulates this twofold prayer of protest: both the
people's protest to God, and God's protest to them. In dramatic and moving stories like the healing of the blind Bartimaeus or of the epileptic demoniac (Mark 10:46–52; 9:14–29),
Jesus receives and responds to the cries of those who have
good reason to believe that God has deserted them, a belief
that was doubtless regularly reinforced by others who were
always glad of an excuse for not having to worry about the
sick or the deprived. Jesus overrides the attempts of those

around him to silence Bartimaeus; and he responds at once to the moving words of the epileptic boy's father, who answers Jesus' comments about the need for faith by crying out: 'I do have faith. Help the little faith I have!' (Mark 9:24).

In so doing, Jesus acts out God's protest against a people who had again forgotten him, and who (as with Jeremiah) now reject or ignore the one who acts as his mouthpiece. But, again like Jeremiah, Jesus suffers more than the rejection of those to whom he has come. He suffers God's rejection too. In Gethsemane St Mark's description of Jesus' prayer makes this uncomfortably explicit:

> They came to a plot of land called Gethsemane; and he said to his disciples, 'Stay here while I pray'. Then he took Peter and James and John with him. And he began to feel terror and anguish. And he said to them, 'My soul is sorrowful to the point of death. Wait here, and stay awake.' And going on a little further he threw himself on the ground and prayed that, if it were possible, this hour might pass him by. 'Abba, Father!' he said, 'For you everything is possible. Take this cup away from me. But let it be as you, not I, would have it.' (Mark 14:32–36)

This crucial passage takes us to the heart of the prayer of protest. The child cries out to its parent ('Abba, Father!') to save it from imminent and appalling suffering. No answer is recorded; and the silence of God at this climactic moment both echoes and addresses the experience of millions whose prayers in the face of suffering appear to have gone unanswered. Dorothée Soelle writes:

> Thus Jesus prayed that he would be spared the agony that lay before him. But to this plea he receives no answer. God is silent, as he has been so often in the history of mankind, and Jesus remains alone with his repeated cry, his fear of death, his insane hope, his threatened life.[2]

What we are to make of that silence depends upon what we make of Jesus' own identity and mission. But perhaps this at least may be said: that Christ in Gethsemane cries out for deliverance from the cup of suffering that earlier he had exhorted his own disciples to drink from (Mark 10:35–40); that here we are presented, not with a calm and untroubled hero readily embracing a martyr's death, but with a deeply human figure instinctively recoiling from the ultimate consequence of what he has said and done, and of how others reacted to it; and yet that in the end that very figure stands firm, and goes forward. We cannot know whether his prayer was answered, though we may believe that it was heard. But we can affirm that the very act of articulating it helped to make possible the action that followed.

This brings us at last to Golgotha, and to the words which may reasonably be said to represent the *locus classicus* of the prayer of protest. The crucified Jesus, inexorably approaching death, cries out in a loud voice the terrible opening words of the twenty-second Psalm: 'My God, my God, why have you forsaken me?' (Mark 15:34). Some have supposed that Jesus or the evangelist had in mind here the whole of that psalm, and that since it ends in triumph the words symbolize Christ's victory. Others, surely rightly, have argued that the words do not read like that:[3] they too are met with silence, and Jesus dies soon after uttering them.

The prayer of protest that ends Jesus' life on earth gathers together all the themes of this chapter. The experience of the divine love, the intimacy of a relationship with his Creator that found natural expression in terms of parental affection – all this was shredded and vanished like the dawn mist in summer, leaving Jesus naked and exposed to the immediate and incredible horror of death by crucifixion. Jesus is recorded as experiencing directly the bizarre disjunction between the trust and mutuality he had once shared with God and the stark silence he now encountered; for even if we assume, with the gospels, that he expected death, there is no good reason to suppose that he expected dereliction too. The darkness that St Mark describes as enshrouding Jesus before he cries out (Mark 15:33) in no way resembles the cloud that cloaked the friend of Moses on the summit of Sinai. It is, simply, darkness, as icy and lifeless as that which covered the deep in the opening words of the Bible. And in it Christ dies.

In the unanswered prayer, the silence, the suffering and the death, the human and divine prayers of protest collide. On the cloud-covered mountain, in the suffering of Israel and supremely at Golgotha, human beings meet a God whose sorrow and protest and dereliction matched their own. By incarnating *that* God, and no other, Christ incarnates too the furthest extremities of human experience, not so as to save us from having to undergo them, but so as to sustain us when we do. For he reveals not only a God *to* whom we pray, but one *with* whom we pray. So our prayer becomes his prayer, our cries of protest his, our gratuitous and useless suffering his as well. And whenever any creature, in gas chambers or hospitals or earthquake-stricken cities, or even in the steel stalls of veal calf pens, cries out in protest at the sick brutality or sheer grinding unfairness of what they experience, Christ prays in and for them, not dispensing the answers but sharing the questions, and making of their suffering God's own summons to a better and juster world.

NOTES

1 I am greatly indebted to the Revd Dr Trevor Dennis for pointing this out to me.
2 Dorothée Soelle, *Suffering*, tr. Kalin (London, DLT, 1975), p. 79.
3 See, e.g., Morna D. Hooker, *The Message of Mark* (London, Epworth, 1983), p. 102.

FURTHER READING

Robert Davidson, *The Courage to Doubt*. London, SCM, 1983.

2

The Garden of Delights
The Song of Songs

As a child, and like most children, I loved playing. My brother and I, with nearby friends, chased each other round the house; constructed dens in rough wooded wasteland; built great castles with toy bricks. Most of all we day-dreamed and imagined: we were the Lone Ranger, or Superman; the little hut in the garden was a palace, or at least a cafe; the garden of the people next door was an intriguing but hostile dominion, requiring investigation and conquest. Bedtime was an infuriating interruption to the latest grand exploit or secret plan.

I remember feeling both surprise and horror when I found that, at school, play was different. It was rigorously this-worldly: the imagination was sharply excluded, and anyone caught day-dreaming was wasting time or letting the side down. It was serious, not in the sense that all play is, but in a quite new way: our play at home had been serious because it challenged the real world and briefly replaced it with an even better one, but school games seemed no more than the realities of this world taken far too seriously. It was unrelentingly competitive; and my stomach soon churned in anticipatory horror at yet again being the butt of general derision when I came last in the relay race, or scored an own goal at football. Worst, of course, was the fact that, whereas at home there were no winners and losers, school games had very definite successes and failures; and I was invariably among the failures. The rich inner world of childish imaginings and fantasies was irretrievably sacrificed to a bleak outer world of school sport where to look a fool was laughable and nothing mattered but winning. I was a child; and I missed my play.

We may appear to have moved a long way from the world of golden calves and Good Friday. In reality however we are looking at the same world through different spectacles. The need and the capacity to play do not end with childhood, as Ronald Knox knew when he praised G. K. Chesterton as someone who 'grew up from manhood into boyhood'. The adult who loses the capacity to play becomes, in the end, a prisoner of his or her unrelenting seriousness, unable to distinguish between the real world and the world of fantasy. The golden calf was play perverted; and Christ, the first April fool, died a victim of humanity's persistent refusal to honour the real meaning of the Sabbath, and find time to play. Earlier civilizations knew well the importance of this: Aristotle, quoting an earlier philosopher, told the readers of his Ethics to 'play, so that you may be serious';[1] and there exists, in traditions as far apart as early Buddhism, classical Graeco-Roman fables and the stories of the desert fathers, a vivid story about the need for even the busiest and cleverest people to play from time to time if they are not to become like an overstretched bow.[2] It is instructive to compare in this regard the recorded sayings of Jesus and St Paul: where Paul tells the Corinthians that he 'gave up childish ways' on becoming a man (1 Cor. 13:11), Jesus positively encouraged his disciples to 'turn and become like children' if they were to enter the kingdom of heaven (Matt. 18:1–4). It is unfair to wrench sayings out of context, but hard to avoid the sneaking feeling that Jesus might have been more at home in the world of childlike enchantment than many of those who have written about him. There are very few activities that are common to almost all creatures, wild and caged, as well as to human beings; but one of them is play. And its continuing importance in the sombre world of late twentieth-century reality is signalled in one of the strangest and most exciting books of the Bible, and the one which, despite its apparently exclusive concern with the celebration of human love, has most influenced Christian spirituality: the Song of Songs.

This extraordinary love poem remains unique among the books of the Bible, partly because of the unparalleled richness and diversity of its vocabulary, and partly because there still exists no scholarly consensus about its origin, date or even its purpose, let alone about how it came to appear in the Jewish scriptures. The greatest Protestant theologian Karl Barth was one of many to see it as the sequel to the story of Eden:

> Genesis 2 is not absolutely isolated in the Old Testament. We might almost speak of a second Magna Carta of humanity in this connexion when we remember that at a rather curious point in the Old Testament canon a place is found for the Song of Songs. We should not wish that this book were not in the canon. And we should not spiritualise it, as if what is in the canon can have only a spiritualised significance. As all honest exposition must admit, and as ought to be recognised gladly rather than with hesitation and embarrassment, it is a collection of genuine love-songs . . .[3]

How is it to be interpreted? And what does it have to do with spirituality, let alone with the spirituality of protest? This passionate and even erotic celebration of human love, purporting to describe in poetry of exquisite beauty the relationship of Solomon and a foreign woman, may appear to have about as much to do with prayer, or even play, as Mrs Beeton. Yet no text has done more to enrich and inform the western spiritual tradition than this. In part, this doubtless reflects the Church's perennial obsession with sex: the best way to neutralize the dangerous suggestiveness of this most sensual of love-poems was to allegorize it, shifting the focus from earth to heaven and quietly anaesthetizing its eroticism in the process. But there are other reasons for its importance. Even as allegory (most commonly as a metaphor for the relationship of God with the human soul), the text is immensely powerful, especially if it is seen (as it surely should be seen) as a kind of sequel to the story of Eden. The best approach to it may perhaps be arrived at by way of an analogy from one of the historical periods most influenced by it: the medieval West.

Much scholarly ink has been spilt over a remarkable treatise written by one Andreas Capellanus (Andrew the Chaplain) in the late twelfth century, and entitled simply *De Amore*. The first two books contain a series of witty and (for its day) extremely radical reflections on love, cutting across both feudal hierarchies and religious taboos. But then the author concludes with a third book that firmly restates traditional Christian and social values and appears to contradict everything he has written thus far. This third book has caused much controversy: some scholars argue that it was added later, perhaps in response to criticism or by some disapproving monk. Neither theory is very probable. The most likely explanation is that of P. G. Walsh who argues that we understand the *De Amore* best if we see its first two books as play: he writes that: 'its author is daringly and humorously discussing in stylised play ideas of love and marriage which have no status in the real world of twelfth-century society, but which challenge and criticise the prevailing mores of sex and marriage imposed by feudal law and Christian precept.'[4]

Precisely this could be said of the Song of Songs, perhaps in its original context, certainly in the way it has been interpreted. The Song of Songs is play: it subverts, for a brief and heady moment, a stern and male-dominated society: it turns a simple woman into the bride of King Solomon, and very much his equal (the relationship between the man and the woman throughout the poem is strikingly free from stereotypes, competitiveness and inequality); it transfigures human love in a relationship which exalts both intimacy and differentness, each person being fulfilled in their mutual self-giving; and it thereby challenges the world and society in which it was written. This is a 'wouldn't-it-be-wonderful-if' approach to reality, a fantasy that contains within itself the seeds of its own fulfilment, and a protest against all that imprisons and confines the human spirit. This element of protest is crucial to the nature of play, among animals and humans alike: polar bear cubs playing king-of-the-castle in a zoo, and children doing something similar on a bleak housing estate, are not just running away from reality: they are keeping alive, in their play, the lost spirit of freedom, acting out in fantasy the way things should be, and thereby helping to ensure that one day they could be. Far from offering a way to escape from the real world, the Song of Songs offers a way to transform it.

The scene that is set in the opening section of the Song appears to suggest the mutual love of King Solomon (to whom the whole work is ascribed, 1:1) and a simple countrywoman (the famous words of the woman 'I am very dark, but comely' (1:5) may, as Michael Goulder argues, imply that the woman is a foreign princess and that, like the book of Jonah, the whole work is a universalist statement of God's love for foreigners as well as for Jews; but the argument is not conclusive.)[5] It is significant that the woman has the first words (1:2–7), and that their devotion to each other is entirely reciprocated.

There is no coherent narrative in the Song, though two sections (2:8 to 3:5 and 5:2 to 6:3) contain the outline of a story. In each case the theme is the same: the man comes seeking his beloved, inviting her to respond to him; when she does so, he mysteriously vanishes, and her frantic search for him is at first unsuccessful. Then, just as mysteriously, he reappears, and their love is consummated. The poetry here is of extraordinary delicacy and beauty, and the Authorized Version captures it to perfection:

> My beloved spake, and said unto me, Rise up, my love,
> my fair one, and come away.
> For lo, the winter is past, the rain is over and gone;
> The flowers appear on the earth; the time of the singing of
> birds is come, and the voice of the turtle is heard in
> our land;
> The fig tree putteth forth her green figs, and the vines with
> the tender grape give a good smell.
> Arise, my love, my fair one, and come away! (2:10–13)

These two sections frame a central passage (3:6 to 5:1) which celebrates briefly the greatness of King Solomon: this celebration, however, soon gives way to a much longer encomium of his beloved (4:1–15) which culminates in the exquisite central climax:

I come to my garden, my sister, my bride,
I gather my myrrh with my spice,
I eat my honeycomb with my honey,
I drink my wine with my milk.

Eat, O friends, and drink:
drink deeply, O lovers! (5:1)

After the second narrative section, there follows a further
section in which the king praises the beauty of his beloved.
The imagery here is of the most extravagant eroticism, as the
lover describes his beloved from feet to hair:

How graceful are your feet in sandals,
O queenly maiden!
Your rounded thighs are like jewels,
the work of a master hand.
Your navel is a rounded bowl
that never lacks mixed wine.
Your belly is a heap of wheat,
encircled with lilies.
Your two breasts are like two fawns,
twins of a gazelle.
Your neck is like an ivory tower.
Your eyes are pools in Heshbon,
by the gate of Bath-Rabbim.
Your nose is like a tower of Lebanon,
overlooking Damascus.
Your head crowns you like Carmel,
and your flowing locks are like purple;
a king is held captive in the tresses. (7:1–5)

What the bride makes of these almost literally unimaginable
descriptions we are not told; but they appear to have the
desired effect. They go out to the fields and vineyards to
consummate their love (7:11–13); and the Song then moves
swiftly to its tremendous climax, as the bride utters its deepest
truth:

31

> Set me as a seal upon your heart,
> as a seal upon your arm;
> for love is strong as death,
> jealousy as cruel as the grave.
> Its flashes are flashes of fire,
> a most vehement flame.
> Many waters cannot quench love,
> neither can floods drown it.
> If a man offered for love
> all the wealth of his house,
> it would be utterly scorned. (8:6–7)

Yet the work ends, not with grand philosophizing, but with a return to its characteristic style: the lover calls again to his beloved (the reference to gardens, here as throughout the Song, points to its significance as a recovery of the intimate love experienced briefly in Eden):

> O you who dwell in the gardens,
> my companions are listening for your voice;
> let me hear it. (8:13)

And the bride, replying, has the last, magical, word:

> Make haste, my beloved,
> and be like a gazelle or a young stag
> upon the mountains of spices (8:14).

The relationship of lover and beloved is remarkable: the vast disparity between royalty and foreign or peasant woman is entirely annulled by the mutuality of their love. The woman in fact might almost be said to be dominant, were it not for the haunting passages in the two narrative sections when she is briefly reduced to despair. The patriarchal society outside their love might almost not exist; and the whole of creation is transformed by their love. The garden is the crucial symbol of this love: Eden's lost equality is here renewed and recovered. And the city stands for the cruel world of inequality and power struggles outside (3:3 and 5:7). This is supremely the language of play – not as escape from the real world but precisely as protest against it: a tremendous rekindling, in the depths of the lovers' imagination, of how the world should be.

Yet what does all this have to do with God, let alone with prayer? Is the Song not best left as a delectable love poem, and not adulterated in the coy Christian ambience of candles and rosaries and the odour of sanctity? On the contrary: it is precisely because of its nature as a celebration of love that it can still exert a creative influence on the work of prayer. It offers us a way of recovering three crucial aspects of human experience: imagination, desire and love.

First and foremost, and like all playful fantasies, the Song of Songs is a work of the imagination. Hugh Lavery has pointed out[6] that religious people have two languages available to them: the language of concept, and the language of image. Concepts are manipulable, and excluding: for those who know the code they can be made to mean whatever you want; for those who do not they are like a castle drawbridge that excludes them from the inner life within. Much formal spirituality is couched in the stern language of concept, abounding with cerebral words like 'justification', 'sin', 'salvation' and the like, containing as much nourishment for the human spirit as some of the old breakfast cereals did for the human body.

But Jesus preferred image to concept. His recorded sayings are steeped in the earthy imagery of everyday Palestine, and his insights incarnated in stories of extraordinary and compelling power: millions for whom organized religion has never held an appeal will remember, and have recourse to, the stories of the Good Samaritan and the Prodigal Son long after any amount of concept-laden catechizing has been entirely forgotten. And no biblical book is more uninhibitedly imaginative, more utterly concept-free, than the Song of Songs. From start to finish it is image-language, not concept-language; indeed it may be said to contain a more vivid and diverse cascade of images than any other book in the Bible. Spirituality has yet to emerge entirely from the thrall of those who put the imagination under a ban, aware of its capacity to distract and divert. The risk, however, is infinitely worth taking. Not everyone concerned with prayer (or play) wants to read books, go on retreats or go to church. But imagination is a gift at everyone's disposal, and sometimes those least afflicted by intellectual pretension are best at putting it to work.

The potential hazards involved in the use of the imagination in prayer may also be precisely its strengths. Unlike conceptual language, images cannot be so easily controlled. Once the imagination is unleashed it is apt to run riot, which is doubtless why so many experts in the spiritual life counsel against using it at all. It is also less easy to systematize, classify or order. The sequences in the Song are often characterized by an accidental, haphazard, spontaneous style, which has been seen as an argument against its literary unity, but which is much more likely to be a reflection of the nature of the love that is described. It is also strikingly true of most of the formative experiences in our lives: we do proceed by sudden flashes of intuition, sudden experiences of pain, disordered kaleidoscopic encounters and reversals, and we need a way of praying that will relate to this. The ordered, structured, intellectually coherent systems of ladders and levels and castles and mental states beloved of so many spiritual giants can often seem dauntingly distant from the world in which most of us live. The rich imaginative world of the Song of Songs may be closer to the daily experience of most of us than a thousand cool conceptual collects.

How can we use it? Each person's imagination is unique, a gift of God in its own right; but a few tentative suggestions might be worth making. Consider first the nature of public prayer and worship. One of the reasons why so many churches are three-quarters empty is surely because neither building nor liturgy does anything much to nourish the imagination. This is not primarily a matter of tradition, though Protestant spirituality, with its reverence for the Word, has perhaps been more suspicious of imaginative fantasy and the use of the senses in worship than Latin Catholicism or Greek Orthodoxy. Yet it need not be so. The appropriate use of children's art; the harnessing of whatever talents in music, art, poetry or other disciplines exist in the local congregation; the careful and corporate creation of an act of worship that touches our senses and kindles our imagination as well as simply engaging our intellect – all these are within the capacity of even the smallest Christian community.

Something similar applies to personal spirituality. If the conceptual language of most formal prayer fails to engage you, try something different. Write a letter to God, drawing on the full rein of your imagination to express how you feel, or what you want to say. Or imagine, before God, your own life or (better still) that of your family and community as well, as you would most like them to be. The experience of Christians in Latin America and elsewhere is eloquent testimony to the creative and sustaining power of the imagination: small groups of people come together to read the Bible and then 'dream dreams' about how things could be, allowing their imaginative capacities full flight in evoking together a vision of the Christian community as God intended it. It would be easy to dismiss such spirituality as nourishing vain illusions and idle fantasies. It would also be wrong, for we will never know how to set about changing the world as it is until or unless we take time to imagine together the world as it should be. To do these things is to play: to enjoy what the Judaeo–Christian tradition calls 'Sabbath time'; and no true fulfilment or maturity is possible without it.

The second important contribution of the Song of Songs to contemporary spirituality is in its emphasis on desire. Marina Warner rightly says of the Song that 'There has never been a more intense communication of the experience of desire'.[7] Desire was once a crucial element in Christian spirituality: the works of St Augustine and St Gregory the Great, to name but two, are full of it. Augustine's great outburst on this theme in one of his sermons on St John's Gospel immediately precedes a quotation from the Song, and beautifully captures its spirit and his: 'Give me a man that loves, and he will feel what I say. Give me one that longs, one that hungers, one that is travelling in this wilderness, and thirsting and panting . . . give such, and he knows what I say . . .'[8] The desire of Eve for Adam that is part of the curse of Eden and symbolic of their lost intimacy, is restored and transfigured in the Song: it is a mutual longing, one for the other. Much modern spirituality, with its bland repression of feeling or imagination of the life of the senses, has little to say about desire, good or bad; and that is a pity. The Song of Songs points the way to a spirituality that takes with utmost seriousness people's deepest longings; and there is no reason why the longing of the lovers for one another may not appropriately stand as a metaphor, say for exiles longing for their homeland or oppressed people for freedom. Nor is there any reason why our inmost needs and desires should not be shared with God, or why we should not from time to time consider with God what they are, and even cry out in angry protest at their loss. Some of them may seem for ever unattainable, like an old person longing for lost youth; some may seem inappropriate or selfish or wrong. Yet we are creatures of desire, as Augustine and the Song of Songs knew: we are created with an infinite desire that only infinite love can satisfy; and in allowing ourselves to lay bare before God our most secret and urgent longings we may at last discover in him the only and ultimate means to fulfil them.

Yet in the end it is love that is the theme of the Song, its impulse and its goal. And the love described is not simply generalized eroticism. It is something much deeper and much more precise than that. The Song is dialogue and reciprocity: above all it is *relational* in the fullest sense; there is genuine mutuality in the relationship of the man and the woman, entirely (in fact extraordinarily) free from stereotype. The relationship is one of equality and differentness: it is, as Michael Fox says, *communion*,[9] and celebrated for its own sake. What this implies for spirituality has preoccupied many writers, not least because it may seem to rule out an interpretation of the Song conceived in terms of the relationship between God and the human soul. Or does it? St Bernard, in his series of eighty-six sermons on the Song, again and again stands on the verge of affirming that, in love, God and human beings become in some senses equal; and it was precisely this theme in the Song of Songs that led him, in his great twenty-third sermon, to conceive of our relationship with God in three ascending stages: we encounter first the teaching God in the schoolroom; then the judging God in the law court; and finally the loving God in the bedroom. It is the bedroom that forms the high point of his spirituality, the place where God longs to make love to us, and where, in a highly structured society, hierarchies and differences are broken down. This sermon forms one of the high points in medieval spirituality; and the Song of Songs is directly its inspiration.

The love of the two persons is not introverted even if it is often interior. It is transforming and inclusive: other people (represented in the poem by a kind of chorus) are brought in to share it. Furthermore it affects their view of the world around them: the fact that, as the *Encyclopaedia Judaica* soberly points out, the Song contains in eight chapters forty-nine words that appear nowhere else in the Bible, points to the delight taken by the lovers in creation. This love is nevertheless sought for its own sake, requiring no further justification: it is not a celebration of procreation or of marriage, though allusion is made to both of these. It is, as St Bernard also points out, offered unconditionally, free from self-interest, and responded to in the same spirit.[10] In some respects this might seem problematic: it could, for example, smack of the self-indulgent; and it offers little guidance on vexatious ethical issues such as mutual fidelity or sexual activity outside of a single primary relationship. Yet these are issues that the writer is not directly concerned to explore. What the writer does explore is the nature, experience and transforming power of self-giving and mutual love; and in so doing he or she bequeathed to the world an eloquent protest against all that prostitutes or depreciates it.

A final point needs to be made, not least because it returns us to the central theme of this book. The Song is not just a celebration of love, not simply a playful fantasy about relationships as they could be in blithe disregard for the way they generally are. The poem is not just about love: it is also about death. The grim passages already alluded to, where the beloved has to let go of her lover and seek him in despair, are not extraneous details to the poet's grand design; and the final peroration, where love is described as being 'strong as

death', is not empty rhetoric. At the heart of all love is the
experience of death, of letting-go: the king has to let go his
royal power in order to become 'the gazelle on the mountains
of spices'; and the woman has to experience, even – indeed
precisely – at the epicentre of their mutual lovemaking, the
terrible reality of loss:

> My beloved put his hand to the latch,
> and my heart was thrilled within me.
> I arose to open to my beloved,
> and my hands dripped with myrrh,
> my fingers with liquid myrrh,
> upon the handles of the bolt.
> I opened to my beloved,
> but my beloved had turned and gone . . .
> I sought him, but found him not;
> I called him, but he gave no answer.
> The watchmen found me,
> as they went about in the city;
> they beat me, they wounded me,
> they took away my mantle,
> those watchmen of the walls.
> I adjure you, O daughters of Jerusalem,
> if you find my beloved,
> that you tell him
> I am sick with love. (5:4–8)

Love, in the Song of Songs, is not just as strong as death: it
actually *is* death, acnowledged and in the end overcome.
The condition of all genuine love is this desperately difficult
willingness to let go, not once but over and over again: to let
go of the stereotypes and expectations that bind lover and
beloved in crippling straitjackets; to let go of your control,
and even in some senses of your claim upon the other person;
to let them be free to be themselves, and you to be yourself.
At such moments the prayer of protest contains the character
not of play but of tragedy, for personal desire or need may
be in terrible collision with the sovereign dictates of self-giving
love; and our prayer may then be, not a happy celebration,

but a scream of excruciating agony in outraged protest against a God who appears to allow all our hopes and longings to be so cruelly and unfairly disappointed. Not the least of the contributions of the Song of Songs to spirituality is precisely its readiness to face this reality without flinching:

> For love is strong as death,
> jealousy is cruel as the grave.
> Its flashes are flashes of fire,
> a most vehement flame. (8:6)

The way of love is a constant series of little deaths; and physical death is only the ultimate letting-go in the face and the hope of the ultimate receiving.

And that is why this rich and playful fantasy is so indispensable to genuine spirituality: because like all the best fantasies it turns out in the end to be true – not in the literal sense of historical reality but in the much deeper sense of offering a way of looking at life that is authentic, that works. C. S. Lewis wrote that, when children read about enchanted woods, they do not begin to despise the real woods: rather 'the reading makes all real woods a little enchanted'.[11] The prayer of protest, the harnessing of imaginative fantasy and innermost desires in the search for meaning and wholeness, is both playful and deeply serious, summoning us not just to challenge the bleak realities of life but to change them – and ourselves – by seeing them as they really are, and by bringing to bear upon them all our lost or stunted capacities for play, fantasy, imagination and wonder. If we cannot or will not do this we will become prisoners of our massive, bustling seriousness, our receptive senses atrophied, our relationships pickled in artificial preservatives, and our sense of God arid and remote. If we can, we may be surprised to find our attitude to life slowly and subtly shifting. Some of the things we had always been obsessive about may turn out not to matter very much after all. Some of the people we had always despised may, to our infuriated amazement, have something to teach us. Some of the experiences we had most dreaded may instead prove unexpectedly rewarding. And it may be at such a moment that the God who made us to play with him in Eden reveals the most surprising truth of all: that the beloved in the Song of Songs is each one of us; that *we* are failures and yet beautiful; and that, just when we least expected it, the greatest of all lovers is tapping on our window.

NOTES

1 Aristotle, *Ethics*, tr. Thomson (London, Penguin, 1955), p. 302.
2 For the Buddhist version see the *Dhammapada*, tr. Mascaro (London, Penguin, 1973), p. 25. For the classical version see Phaedrus, *Fables*, tr. Parry (Heinemann, Loeb Classical Library, 1965), Book 3.14. It also appears in *Sayings of the Desert Fathers*, tr. Ward (London, Mowbrays, 1975), p. 3.
3 *Church Dogmatics*, vol. III Part 2, ed. T. and T. Clark (English tr., 1960), p. 294.
4 P. G. Walsh in introduction to *Andreas Capellanus on Love* (Duckworth, 1982), p. 6.
5 Michael Goulder, *The Song of Fourteen Songs*. Sheffield University Press, 1986.
6 'The priest and presence' in *Spirituality and Priesthood*, Supplement to *The Way*, Summer 1983.
7 *Alone of all her Sex* (Quartet, 1978), p. 126.
8 *Sermons on the Gospel of St John*, 26.4.
9 Michael Fox, *The Song of Songs and the Ancient Egyptian Love Songs* (Wisconsin University Press, 1985), p. 322.
10 *Sermons on the Song of Songs*, 83.5
11 *On Three Ways of Writing for Children*, quoted in R. K. Johnston, *The Christian at Play* (Grand Rapids, Eerdmans, 1983), p. 76.

FURTHER READING

Marvin Pope, *Song of Songs*. New York, Anchor Bible Commentary, 1977.
Francis Landy, *Paradoxes of Paradise: identity and difference in the Song of Songs*. Sheffield, Almond Press, 1983.
Michael Goulder, *The Song of Fourteen Songs*. Sheffield University Press, 1986.
Marcia Falk, *Love Lyrics from the Bible: a translation and literary study of the Song of Songs*. Sheffield, Almond Press, 1982.

The Garden of Delights

Michael V. Fox, *The Song of Songs and the Ancient Egyptian Love Songs*.
Wisconsin University Press, 1985.

3

The Waters of the Deep
The Psalms and the Book of Job

On 24 June 1984 I awoke with a pain in my stomach. It would be more accurate to say I lay awake, because by that time the pain I had first sensed two days earlier had become sufficiently severe to make sleep almost impossible. Even so it was a dull ache rather than a sharp stabbing pain. It was a Sunday morning and I was a vicar. Vicars are important people on Sunday mornings, and I had work to do. At about 7 a.m., pandering (as always) to the hallowed doctrine of the indispensability of clergymen, I began to get dressed.

It was a bad move. I started to think about the morning's sermon, expecting such godly thoughts to drive away all worldly cares such as pains in your stomach. They did not. I sat to say my morning prayers, confidently assuming that the Te Deum would be enough to demolish the after-effects of indigestion. It was not. It was not indigestion either, and an appalling thought began at last to dawn in my busy, self-important, organizing mind. There are some things that take precedence even over the lofty privilege of leading the people of God in worship. This was one of them.

I had acute appendicitis: in less than an hour the busy vicar, about to preside at the Sunday Eucharist, was transformed into an almost-naked figure on a stretcher in a casualty waiting room. It is difficult to express what this felt like, and easy to exaggerate with hindsight: I was not after all being confronted with a life-threatening illness or with the prospect of prolonged disability. But it was traumatic enough for me, unaccustomed as I was to sickness of any kind. Worst was the sudden and complete lack of control over my own life: like many active and articulate middle-class people I had

42

come to take that for granted. I was, and am, a child of a society where the waiting had been taken out of the wanting – for all but the disadvantaged. From instant credit to instant coffee I had and did what I wanted when I wanted. I had exerted an amazing degree of control over every aspect of my life – until 24 June 1984.

It was an utterly bewildering experience, reversing almost every previous certainty. I fretted: how on earth would they cope back in the church without me? (They did, of course, effortlessly, vicars being far less important than they like to suppose.) What were they going to do to me, and when? How long would I be out of action? Would it hurt? In the turmoil I picked up the only book that had accompanied me, thrown hastily into a small case with pyjamas and the like. It was what I had been reading earlier in a vain attempt to dispel the stomach-ache, and contained the assortment of ancient religious poems or hymns that comprise the Book of Psalms. I looked up the psalm appointed for that day, the feast of St John the Baptist, and read:

> I love the Lord, because he has heard
> the voice of my supplication,
> because he has inclined his ear to me
> whenever I called upon him.
> The cords of death entangled me;
> the grip of the grave took hold of me;
> I came to grief and sorrow.
> Then I called upon the Name of the Lord:
> 'O Lord, I pray you, save my life.' (Ps. 116:1–4)

The mix of eager hope and urgent prayer, seasoned with imagery that spoke directly to my unexpected predicament, touched the parts of me that other prayers could never have reached: my fear of pain, of losing control or status or good health; my chaotic, disordered powerlessness. Later I discovered that this was one of the psalms Jesus would have said with his disciples immediately before entering Gethsemane (Matt. 26:30). The 116th psalm offered no instant answer, dispelled no pain and restored no power. What it did offer was a way of expressing how I felt, of identifying with millions who had trodden this way before me, and of making contact with one who had once made that way his own. That was all; but it was enough.

The Psalms are the seedbed of all Jewish and Christian prayer: they are also a manual of contemporary spirituality as appropriate to the inner city as to any ancient synagogue. Though remarkably little is known even now about their origins, or about how or when they were used, this much at least seems to be clear: they served both for private prayer and for public worship; and even those psalms which appear most deeply and intimately personal have a certain formulaic character which makes it clear that they were never intended simply to express one person's experience, but rather to articulate that of the whole community, and of anyone who had undergone something similar. This is a point of crucial importance: even at their most intensely introverted, the Psalms are always also corporate prayers, articulating the mind and story of whole communities as well as of isolated individuals. This is true both of their earliest use and of the way they have always been prayed. Whenever you use one, whether at home alone or at evening prayer in a cathedral, or as part of a small monastic community chanting them rhythmically in the silent reaches of the night, the whole Church prays with you: your anger is her anger, your longing or lonely needs hers, your tiny act of puny thanksgiving part of the lifeblood of the people of God, your unseen cry of protest caught up and consecrated by the murdered Christ who prayed those words before you did, and prays them with you now. The Psalms are holy ground, not only (or even primarily) because of the millions of Jews and Christians who have been provoked and excited and sustained by them, but also because the words and images are themselves sacraments lifting you into a deeper identification with the God to whom you call, and the people with or for whom you pray. You never pray them on your own. John Cassian, writing for monks in the early fifth century, expresses this well:

The good man will sing [the Psalms] no longer as verses

composed by a prophet, but as born of his own prayers . . . There are times when a man understands God's Scriptures with the clarity with which a surgeon understands the body when he opens up the marrow and the veins. These are the times when our experience seems to show us the meaning by practical proof before we understand it intellectually. For example, if we have the same attitudes of heart wherein the Psalmist wrote or sung his psalms, we shall become like the authors and be aware of the meaning before we have thought it out instead of after. The force of the words strikes us before we have rationally examined them. And when we use the words, we remember . . . our own circumstances and struggles, the results of our negligence or earnestness, the mercies of God's providence or the temptations of the devil, the subtle and slippery sins of forgetfulness or human frailty or unthinking ignorance. All these feelings we find expressed in the psalms.[1]

There are other reasons why the Psalms continue to be provocatively and immediately relevant. All human life is contained within them, from the most furious vindictiveness to the most passionate desire. Like the Song of Songs, the language is that of image, not concept – and the imagery is vividly secular, not vapidly sacred. There is no general belief in any fulfilling life beyond death; and this forces the psalmist to confront the problems of injustice, undeserved suffering and death in unequivocally this-worldly terms. The Psalms were written out of first-hand experience, in a world where violent oppression and arbitrary, motiveless tragedy caused people constantly to challenge and doubt received orthodox wisdom: in other words, in a world remarkably like ours.

Above all though, many of the Psalms are prayers of protest both in the sense of bearing witness to, or articulating, human experience and in that of challenging God to do something about it. Here as elsewhere it is important to stress the twofold character of the spirituality of protest. If the Psalms simply recorded people's experience they would be journals or diaries, valuable records of past events or feelings, but no more than that. If on the other hand they were simply prayers divorced from the experiences which had prompted them, they would lose their capacity to address us today and be lost in the mists of past pious effusions. We are apt to assume that because God already knows all about us there is no need for our prayers to begin with a rehearsal of how we feel or what we have experienced. But we are wrong. To pray is to protest, both by bearing honest (and sometimes painful) witness to our present state and by wrestling with God as we seek to make some sense of it, or to move on beyond it. It is in their capacity to do both of these things that the Psalms still offer a way not only to articulate our feelings, but also to transform them.

It is worth indicating briefly some of the areas of human experience which the Psalms address and challenge. St Jerome described them as the 'ballads of the countryside';[2] but his well-aired aversion to city life may have precluded him from perceiving that they are equally songs of the city. Consider the passionate plea of Psalm 55:

> Hear my prayer, O God;
> do not hide yourself from my petition.
> Listen to me and answer me;
> I have no peace, because of my cares . . .
> My heart quakes within me,
> and the terrors of death have fallen upon me.
> Fear and trembling have come over me,
> and horror overwhelms me.
> And I said, 'Oh, that I had wings like a dove!
> I would fly away and be at rest.
> I would flee to a far-off place
> and make my lodging in the wilderness.
> I would hasten to escape
> from the stormy wind and tempest.'
> Swallow them up, O Lord;
> confound their speech;
> for I have seen violence and strife in the city . . .
> There is corruption at her heart;
> her streets are never free of oppression and deceit.
> For had it been an adversary who taunted me,

then I could have borne it;
or had it been an enemy who vaunted himself against me,
then I could have hidden from him.
But it was you, a man after my own heart,
my companion, my own familiar friend.
We took sweet counsel together,
and walked with the throng in the house of God.
Let death come upon them suddenly . . . (55:1–14)

The queasy sentimentality of the setting by Mendelssohn of part of this psalm[3] exemplifies perfectly the way in which the message of the Psalms has been either ignored or transmogrified by successive generations of Christians who have preferred piety to protest. The psalmist writes *de profundis*, from the depths of hopelessness and despair: restlessness and stress give way successively to fear, a longing to escape, a reflection on urban violence, a bitter sense of personal betrayal and a desire for revenge. It is neither difficult nor anachronistic to imagine it as the desperate prayer of a person living in a decaying housing estate and recently mugged or raped by someone they knew.

The terrible fifty-eighth psalm goes even further. Even as a poem the violence and fury of its imagery and message are immensely powerful; as a prayer it is literally breathtaking:

Do you indeed decree righteousness, you rulers?
do you judge the people with equity?
No; you devise evil in your hearts,
and your hands deal out violence in the land.
The wicked are perverse from the womb;
liars go astray from their birth.
They are as venomous as a serpent,
they are like the deaf adder which stops its ears,
which does not heed the voice of the charmer,
no matter how skilful his charming.
O God, break their teeth in their mouths;
pull the fangs of the young lions, O Lord.
Let them vanish like water that runs off;
let them wither like trodden grass.

Let them be like the snail that melts away,
like a stillborn child that never sees the sun . . . (58:1–8)

Those accustomed to thinking of prayer in terms of the bland
sonorities of modern liturgy or the soothing nosegays of Victorian children's hymns may recoil from such uninhibited and
unadulterated anger, and from such a fearful request being
directed to God. But anger is inescapably central to everyone's life, however much it is ignored or repressed; and it
may be precisely our failure as Christians to articulate it, in
its unpasteurised rawness, which conduces to making so much
of our worship colourless and dull. Before you are tempted
to dismiss the fifty-eighth psalm, or to festoon it (as do the
compilers of the Alternative Service Book) with prim square
brackets warning potential pray-ers off the dangerous
material contained within, read it again as the prayer of a
victim of football hooliganism or airline hi-jack; try to
imagine, as you read it, someone known to you who has been
a victim of a gross miscarriage of justice; or someone whose
only child was cut down and killed by a drunken driver
sentenced to a derisory punishment, and whose friends and
neighbours constantly criticize them for 'not being able to let
sleeping dogs lie'; let it help you to identify with what it must
feel like to be in such a situation, or to bring to mind an
occasion when you have felt like that yourself; and offer it as
a prayer, not for vengeance, but for justice. The fifty-eighth
psalm remains too as an indictment of all who 'hold divine
power' and abuse it in the lives of helpless and nameless
victims; and its recitation, in the century of Dachau, Hirosh-
ima and the Stalinist purges, is as painful and eloquent a
reminder as the symphonies of Shostakovich or the novels of
Isaac Bashevis Singer, of what they felt and of how much
they endured.

No other psalm compares with this in the sheer ferocity of
its language or anger; but many others address aspects of the
contemporary (indeed the universal) human experience, and
express them in prayer. Psalm 10 begins with a quintessential
prayer of protest, both articulating the experience of power-

48

lessness that constantly characterizes the poor, and challenging God to do something about it:

>Why do you stand so far off, O Lord,
>and hide yourself in time of trouble?
>The wicked arrogantly persecute the poor . . .
>[they] are so proud that they care not for God. (10:1–4)

Psalm 59 might be the prayer of an elderly person terrified of vandals. There is nothing she can do, and no one to whom she can turn. To invite her to pray might smack of the worst kind of religious escapism; but it would not be so if the prayer were the lonely protest of the fifty-ninth psalm:

>Rescue me from my enemies, O God;
>protect me from those who rise up against me.
>Rescue me from evildoers
>and save me from those who thirst for my blood.
>See how they lie in wait for my life,
>how the mighty gather together against me;
>not for any offence or fault of mine, O Lord.
>Not because of any guilt of mine
>they run and prepare themselves for battle . . .
>They go to and fro in the evening;
>they snarl like dogs and run about the city.
>Behold, they boast with their mouths,
>and taunts are on their lips;
>'For who,' they say, 'will hear us?' . . .
>My eyes are fixed on you, O my Strength;
>for you, O God, are my stronghold. (59:1–8)

Psalm 71 is the prayer of an elderly person worried about the sharp disjunction between past blessings and an ominous present:

>For you are my hope, O Lord God,
>my confidence since I was young . . .
>Do not cast me off in my old age;
>forsake me not when my strength fails. (71:5, 8–9)

The psalms are concerned not only with individual experience but with that of whole communities, or of the entire nation. The most striking example of this is the long Psalm 89, two-thirds of which consists of an apparently untroubled celebration of God's providential care for his people. Then with devastating abruptness the mood changes:

> But you have cast off and rejected your anointed;
> you have become enraged at him.
> You have broken your covenant with your servant,
> defiled his crown, and hurled it to the ground. (89:38–39)

The conclusion wrestles with this appalling problem: what has happened to the God who made a solemn covenant with his people? Why has he suddenly deserted them? The protest is expressed in a forceful reminder to God of his obligations to his chosen people, a reminder which might seem unattractive or even presumptuous to us until we remember the times in our own lives when we have been driven to cry out, 'Why? What have I done to deserve this?' or simply, 'This is an intolerable outrage!' We may not share the Israelite sense of being a chosen nation, or a view of providence which appears to assume that everything which happens is directly caused and intended by God; but we must surely share their sense of confusion and protest when tragedy strikes. It is, as will be seen, a theme that receives fuller treatment in the Book of Job.

First though, it is worth pursuing slightly further the expressions of protest to be found in the Psalms. It is striking to discover in them many of the characteristic features of present-day experience of depression or stress: a sense of being trapped, graphically expressed in the nightmarish imagery of drowning:

> Save me, O God,
> for the waters have risen up to my neck.
> I am sinking in deep mire,
> and there is no firm ground for my feet. (69:1–2)

In sleeplessness and agonizing doubt:

> You will not let my eyelids close;
> I am troubled and I cannot speak . . .
> I commune with my heart in the night;
> I ponder and search my mind . . .
> Will the Lord cast me off for ever?
> will he no more show his favour? (77:4–7)

In endless crying:

> I grow weary because of my groaning;
> every night I drench my bed
> and flood my couch with tears. (6:6)

In a crippling sense of guilt:

> My iniquities overwhelm me;
> like a heavy burden they are too much
> for me to bear. (38:4)

A fearful isolation:

> I look to my right hand
> and find no one who knows me;
> I have no place to flee to,
> and no one cares for me. (142:4)

A terrible sense of rejection, even by friends . . .

> I have become a reproach
> to all my enemies
> and even to my neighbours,
> a dismay to those of my acquaintance;
> when they see me in the street they avoid me.
> I am forgotten like a dead man, out of mind;
> I am as useless as a broken pot. (31:11)

. . . and worst of all, by God:

Lord, why have you rejected me?
   why have you hidden your face from me? . . .
My friend and my neighbour you have put away from me,
   and darkness is my only companion. (88:15,19)

This last psalm is the most uncompromising and moving evocation of darkness and hopelessness to be found in the psalter; it could be the prayer of a leper, or that of someone suffering from AIDS who gradually discovers that all his or her so-called Christian friends suddenly, and with infinitely convincing excuses, don't want to know him any more when they find out what is wrong. This is the prayer of protest in its starkest and most authentic form; and such hope as it embodies is to be found not in any hint of a happy ending but simply in the fact that it is *there*, that it can still be prayed, even though the answer seems only to be infinite silence. At the ultimate extremity of human experience, beyond the reach of most prayers and the imaginings of most people, the eighty-eighth psalm might still incarnate the deepest feelings of those who are living 'on the edge', and might still remind the rest of us that we are one with them.

Yet the prayer of protest in the Psalms is more than the painful expression of personal or corporate experience, more than a cry to God to hear and respond. It is also a challenge to belief, a protest against the easy cliches of received religious wisdom. In this regard the most remarkable in the collection is Psalm 73, which begins with an apparent statement of faith:

Truly, God is good to Israel,
   to those who are pure in heart. (73:1)

But it abruptly becomes clear that there is a great gulf between this pious recitation of orthodoxy and the psalmist's actual experience. God rewards his own, he looks after the pure in heart, he punishes the wicked . . . But wait a moment! That is simply untrue, as the psalmist proceeds to make clear – the 'yet' of verse 2 sharply contradicting the smooth simplicity of verse 1:

But as for me, my feet had nearly slipped;
I had almost tripped and fallen;
Because I envied the proud
and saw the prosperity of the wicked. (73:2–3)

Far from getting punished, the wicked do very well indeed,
as the psalmist graphically observes:

For they suffer no pain,
and their bodies are sleek and sound;
In the misfortunes of others they have no share;
they are not afflicted as others are;
Therefore they wear their pride like a necklace
and wrap their violence about them like a cloak. (73:4–6)

These are the powerful, the rich, those ready either directly
or indirectly to preserve their way of life by violence and
oppression. The terrible thing is that they get away with it.
So it isn't surprising that people turn and follow them (v.
10), and live their lives without the least reference to God (v.
11). In which case, what point is there in being pure in
heart, asks the psalmist, directly challenging his own opening
statement:

In vain have I kept my heart clean,
and washed my hands in innocence.
I have been afflicted all day long,
and punished every morning. (73:13–14)

At this point something extraordinary happens. The psalmist
appears to falter:

Had I gone on speaking this way,
I should have betrayed the generation
    of your children.
When I tried to understand these things,
it was too hard for me;

> Until I entered the sanctuary of God
> and discerned the end of the wicked. (73:15–17)

These verses deserve a closer look. Notice first the way the psalmist argues with himself, struggling with the appalling disjunction between what he has been taught to believe and what squares with his own experience. This is the articulation not simply of protest but also of doubt. It is precisely in their capacity to confront the questions all of us ask from time to time, and many people all of the time, that the Psalms address the human condition: our inner selves, our half-conscious doubts and anxieties and uncertainties that so much religious utterance or worship is apt to sweep ruthlessly under the carpet. If the Psalms refuse easy answers, they certainly help us to acknowledge the questions.

The psalmist, then, is in an agonizing dilemma, torn between his indebtedness to those who have gone before him and his own present experience. He struggles wth the question; he wrestles with his doubts 'in the sanctuary of God'. Too many sanctuaries of God exude effortless and complacent certainty in so far as they exude anything at all. God forbid that we should turn our churches into grim evocations of only the darker side of human experience; but God deliver us from the compulsory heartiness and plastic jollification that all too often passes for genuine prayer or worship. This is not to say that prayer must always be gloomy: however, it is to say that it must always be honest. Prayer, for this psalmist at least, is no effortless recitation of limp platitudes but an active and mature and costly struggle.

The conclusion he reaches is really threefold: first that power and wealth and wickedness are *in the end* no way to fulfilment and no guarantee against disaster; secondly, and more perceptively, that becoming embittered himself (v. 21) could ultimately cut *him* off from God too; and thirdly, and most important of all, that despite his unhappiness and questioning God is still close to him:

> Yet I am always with you;
> you hold me by my right hand . . .

Whom have I in heaven but you?
and having you I desire nothing upon earth.
Though my flesh and my heart
    should waste away,
God is the strength of my heart
    and my portion for ever. (73:23–26)

The initial 'yet' answers the 'but' of verse 2, the initial challenge. The psalmist is not withdrawing his challenge: if he had, the psalm would never have stayed in the collection. What he comes to see is that God loves and sustains him in and through it. True wholeness is experienced, not in the barren arrogance of the powerful, but in the lonely questions and fragile trust of the weak. And the psalm ends on a note of praise:

But it is good for me to be near God;
I have made the Lord God my refuge.
I will speak of all your works
in the gates of the city of Zion. (73:27–29)

This striking collision, within one psalm, of protest and intimacy, of a sense of doubt and a sense of God's loving presence, points to a crucial aspect of the prayer of protest, and one that is explored in later chapters: its close relationship with the prayer of love, and with what in Christian spirituality is sometimes known as the unitive way, or the way that leads towards the ultimate union of the human soul with its Creator. As we saw in Chapter 1, the relationship between them is grounded in the cross, for the God who seeks and loves us and calls us to intimate union with himself is also and precisely the dying Christ whose scream of dereliction and protest found expression in the terrible words of Psalm 22: 'My God, my God, why have you forsaken me?' (v. 1) The doubt, anguish and even raging anger which the Book of Psalms supremely embodies need not be obstacles on the journey from humanity to God: honestly acknowledged and expressed they may even become indispensable staging-posts on the way, sources at once of suffering and of hope.

55

Nowhere does such prayer find as eloquent and searching an expression as it is given in the Book of Job, and a study of this kind would be incomplete without at least some reflection on its significance. In its exploration of the problem of undeserved suffering, the book presents us (as Gustavo Gutierrez has recently pointed out)[4] with what are in effect two ways of 'doing theology': on the one hand are Job's friends, who come ostensibly to comfort him after the loss of his family and possessions and whose religious faith begins with external doctrinal principles which are then rigidly applied to human experience; on the other is Job himself, who proceeds in reverse, arguing not from belief to experience, but from experience to belief. Eliphaz, the first of the friends, even argues that God will only hear Job's prayer when he abandons his protest and accepts piously what has befallen him:

> Agree with God, and be at peace;
> thereby good will come to you . . .
> If you return to the Almighty and humble yourself . . .
> then you will delight yourself in the Almighty,
> and lift up your face to God.
> You will make your prayer to him,
> and he will hear you. (22:21–27 RSV)

But Job will have none of this. His prayer is the direct articulation of his experience; and even though he appears at first to seek God in vain (23:3–9) he neither gives up the search nor moderates the fury of his protest. And it is not just his protest but that of all victims of unjust suffering whose prayers the inscrutable Creator appears to ignore:

> From out of the city the dying groan,
> and the soul of the wounded cries for help;
> yet God pays no attention to their prayer. (24:12)

More directly even than the psalmist, Job confronts the central dilemma of the God-fearer: why does God, who wills and controls all things, allow innocent people to suffer? He explores in turn each possibility: could there be limits to God's omnipotence? No, he decides, for:

> He stretches out the north over the void,
> and hangs the earth upon nothing . . .
> The pillars of heaven tremble,
> and are astounded at his rebuke.
> By his power he stilled the sea . . . (26:7,11–12)

Could it be, then, that he is not as innocent as he supposes, and that, as the friends relentlessly maintain, he deserves all he has got? No; that too does not square with his experience, or his memory, as Job recalls in poetry of enormous pathos and power:

> Oh, that I were as in the months of old,
> as in the days when God watched over me;
> when his lamp shone upon my head,
> and by his light I walked through darkness;
> as I was in my autumn days,
> when the friendship of God was upon my tent;
> when the Almighty was yet with me,
> when my children were about me;
> when my steps were washed with milk,
> and the rock poured out for me streams of oil! . . .
> I put on righteousness, and it clothed me;
> my justice was like a robe and a turban.
> I was eyes to the blind,
> and feet to the lame.
> I was a father to the poor,
> and I searched out the cause of him
> whom I did not know. (29:2–6,14–16)

In the end Job goes alone and unrepentant to meet a God who is both judge and prosecutor, and whose inexplicable actions demand an answer. They get one too, in the form of two speeches that together comprise what must be one of the greatest pieces of poetry ever written. But what kind of an answer is it? In a carefully argued textual analysis Robert

Alter has shown[5] how the speeches of God mirror and respond precisely to those of Job and his friends, replacing both the inherited religious orthodoxy of the friends and the deeply felt but inevitably anthropocentric protest of Job with the cosmic paradox that lies at the heart of all creation. It is as though God says to Job: look at things from my perspective, at a world where animals are allowed to go free, like the ass (39:5); but in which they may use that freedom to hurt or kill others, as the lion does in providing for its young (38:39). That is the way the world is, a world where the freedom of creatures to do as they wish can be had only at the cost and risk of unjust suffering being wrought upon the innocent.

Job is not comforted; but he is vindicated. After all his terrible accusations and protests, God commends Job for speaking the truth about him (42:7), and castigates the friends for not doing the same. The protagonists of barren and gloomy orthodoxy are in the end forgiven only through the prayers of Job (42:8): the lonely protester becomes a redemptive figure, anticipating one whose cry of protest on a cross was to herald the world's healing. And there is more: the religious outcast, struggling to find the God who seemed to have deserted him, sees God with his own eyes (42:5): received piety is replaced by intimate personal experience; and the prayer of doubt and protest is, in the extremity of suffering, transformed into a divine encounter.

How can we make such a prayer our own? The wholesale adoption of the psalter or the Book of Job as the exclusive spiritual diet of contemporary humanity would offer no solution, for such texts are creatures of their own day and, for all their honesty and power, they may on occasions speak with or presuppose a world-view that millions could no longer hold. Yet the imaginative recitation of the Psalms has remained part of the essence of Jewish and Christian spirituality throughout the centuries. They can be used as means of identifying, in prayer, with those who suffer or protest; means of articulating, also in prayer, your own chaotic or half-acknowledged experience or deepest longings; means of addressing issues and problems that are all too easily submerged or brushed aside. To do these things may sometmes require sensitive and appropriate shifts in meaning. It can, for example, be effective to think of the 'wicked' or the 'enemies' that appear so frequently not as external agents but as all that assails or clogs or oppresses you from within: we need reminding, from time to time, that spirituality is not only about communion or compassion: it is also about confrontation with the powers of evil, powers that exist and are active not only 'out there' but deep within each one of us; and using the texts in this way can help to make sense of passages in otherwise deeply intimate and personal prayers like Psalm 139 or Psalm 63 where the references to evil or enemies can come as an unwelcome shock. It can transform the impact of a psalm, too, if you allow yourself to imagine situations or people for whom it might speak: the haunting Psalm 42, for example, makes a searching and eloquent prayer for a priest or minister working or living under stress, and the tiny Psalm 134 a simple act of prayer to close the day. Neither the Psalms nor the Book of Job are simply prayers of protest or anger or doubt; indeed to read or pray through the psalter is to engage with almost every aspect of human experience and feeling, from desperate suffering to uninhibited joy. And that is precisely the point.

For these great expressions of the deepest human experiences, for all their cultural limitations and differences, offer us a model for all Christian prayer and worship: they are, simply, sacraments, points of encounter between our own muddled and kaleidoscopic experience of life, and the God who is present at its very heart. No experience, or creature, is too tiny or too trivial to count in this process of bringing our lives and our world into collision with the God who sustains them; and we should beware of the temptation to blunt the cutting-edge of that collision by excluding the earthy or anaesthetizing the emotional. It is not insignificant, for example, that the vital and vivid Psalm 104, effectively a blueprint for 'green' prayer with its colourful celebration of rabbits, sea-monsters and wild mountain goats, is customarily experienced in Anglican worship only in the anodyne pomposity of Sir Robert Grant's paraphrase 'O worship the King', which replaces all the sparkling images of the original with the words: 'This earth, with its store of wonders untold . . .' For us, as for Job, prayer that does not begin with the world as it is will never help us to transform it into the world as it should be. The prayer of protest is only a part of a wider dialectic, a way of praying that seeks to bring all life into an encounter with its Creator; and by making such prayer our own we may catch glimpses of a wholeness and maturity that is accessible by no other or easier way. The prayer of protest and the prayer of intimate love are in the end one:

Answer me when I call, O God, defender of my cause;
you set me free when I am hard-pressed;
have mercy on me and hear my prayer . . .
You have put gladness in my heart,
more than when grain and wine and oil increase.
I lie down in peace; at once I fall asleep;
for only you, Lord, make me dwell in safety. (Ps. 4:1,7–8)

NOTES

1 Cassian, 'Conferences' 10.11, tr. Owen Chadwick in *Western Asceticism*, vol. X in Library of Christian Classics (Philadelphia, 1958), pp. 243–4.
2 St Jerome, Epistle 46.12.
3 The setting of 'O for the wings of a dove' forms part of Mendelssohn's anthem 'Hear my prayer' (1844).
4 Gutierrez, *On Job*, esp. pp. 21ff.
5 See Robert Alter, *The Art of Biblical Poetry* (New York, Basic Books, 1985), ch. IV.

FURTHER READING

Psalms

Walter Brueggemann, *The Message of the Psalms*. Augsburg Old Testament Studies, Minneapolis, 1984.

Walter Brueggemann, *Praying the Psalms*. Winona, Minn., St Mary's Press, 1982.

C. S. Lewis, *Reflections on the Psalms*. 1958.

Peter Ackroyd, *Doors of Perception: a guide to reading the Psalms*. London, SCM, 1978.

Laurence Dunlop, *Patterns of Prayer in the Psalms*. New York, Seabury Press, 1982.

John H. Eaton, *The Psalms Come Alive*. London, Mowbrays, 1984.

Maria Boulding, *Marked for Life: prayer in the Easter Christ* (esp. ch. 6). London, SPCK, 1979.

Thomas Merton, *Bread in the Wilderness*. London, Burns & Oates, 1954, repr. 1976.

Andre Louf, *Teach Us to Pray* (esp. ch. 5). London, DLT, 1974.

Dermot Cox, *The Psalms in the Life of God's People*. Slough, St Paul Publications, 1984.

Book of Job

Harold S. Kushner, *When Bad Things Happen to Good People*. London, Pan, 1982.

Gustavo Gutierrez, *On Job: God-talk and the suffering of the innocent*. Maryknoll, NY, Orbis, 1987.

Norman C. Habel, *The Book of Job* (commentary). London, SCM Old Testament Library series, 1985.

General

Robin Green, *Only Connect: worship and liturgy from the perspective of pastoral care*. London, DLT, 1987. (On relating human experience to worship.)

The Psalms quoted in this chapter are from the Book of Common Prayer of the Episcopal Church of the United States of America. New York, Seabury Press, 1977.

4

The Burning Fiery Furnace
Spirituality and the Apocalypse

Most of us cherish the memory of times, real or imagined, when we have been able to defy the overwhelming might of established authority with our own puny power, and to emerge triumphant. When such moments occur in the life of communities or nations they inevitably acquire a stature and a mythology out of all proportion to the event itself: the story of Pope Leo the Great defying the Vandal army at the gates of Rome, of Joan of Arc rallying the French in the Hundred Years War, or of Rosa Parkes igniting the smouldering anger of blacks in the southern United States by occupying a bus seat reserved for whites, are all classic examples. The Bible is full of such incidents – David and Goliath, Elijah and the prophets of Baal, Judith and Holofernes, Gideon and the Midianites, and supremely Christ before Pilate: indeed there are so many that one may be tempted to surmise a quiet divine preference for the underdog, for anyone confronted with overwhelming odds. And of these stories none is so invigorating as the tale told in the third chapter of the Book of Daniel: the story of the burning fiery furnace.

The story is a narrative masterpiece told with sparkling freshness and colour. King Nebuchadnezzar of Babylon erects a golden statue and commands all his subjects to bow down and worship it as soon as they hear the court band strike up. Those who refuse are to be cast into the burning fiery furnace, victims of the whimsical brutality typical of a tyrant. Three devout and prominent Jews (Shadrach, Meshach and Abed-Nego) refuse to compromise their own beliefs by obeying the royal decree, and are at once reported to the king – a further characteristic of all oppressive regimes is the way they encour-

age their subjects to inform on each other. Nebuchadnezzar
is not amused; and the offenders are summoned. The confrontation between them is a *locus classicus* for all apocalyptic
spirituality:

> Nebuchadnezzar addressed them, 'Shadrach, Meshach and
> Abed-Nego, is it true that you do not serve my gods, and
> that you refuse to worship the golden statue I have set up?
> When you hear the sound of horn, pipe, lyre, zither, harp,
> bagpipe and every other kind of instrument, are you pre
> pared to prostrate yourselves and worship the statue I have
> made? If you refuse to worship it, you will be thrown
> forthwith into the burning fiery furnace; then which of the
> gods could save you from my power?' Shadrach, Meshach
> and Abed-Nego replied to King Nebuchadnezzar, 'Your
> question needs no answer from us: if our God, the one we
> serve, is able to save us from the burning fiery furnace and
> from your power, Your Majesty, he will save us; and even
> if he does not, then you must know, O King, that we will
> not serve your god or worship the statue you have set up.'
> (3:14–18)

The story promptly races to its conclusion: the three are
thrown bound into the fire, in the midst of which (in some
early texts) they chant the great canticle of praise known as
the *Benedicite, omnia opera*. Then the king springs to his feet in
amazement: there, in the heart of the burning fiery furnace,
the three victims who had been thrown in bound fast were
walking about freely; and with them was a fourth, shadowy
figure, who 'looks like a child of the gods' (3:25). Out they
come, unscathed, and the king himself declares what was
doubtless intended as the moral: 'there is no other god who
can save like this' (3:29).

For our purposes, however, the real moral comes earlier.
the answer of Shadrach, Meshach and Abed-Nego to King
Nebuchadnezzar is one of the great moments in scripture:
they do not know whether their god will save them from the
burning fiery furnace. They do not know whether he *can* save
them. But even if he does not, if they die in agony, they will

still not bow down and worship the golden statue. Faith in brute power is met and defeated, on its own ground, by faith in little more than the faintest hope of divine intervention. What demolishes Nebuchadnezzar is not the cool, effortless confidence of the strong, but precisely the fearful and uncertain hope of the weak. Yet such hope not only leads its adherents through the burning fiery furnace, but also enables them to discover a shadowy divine companion in there with them. They do not simply survive the furnace: they are liberated in its very heart.

The Book of Daniel is a work of apocalyptic: the word means 'revelation' or 'unveiling'. It was written in the middle of the second century BCE to encourage the Jews during the persecution of Antiochus Epiphanes, and specifically to counsel resistance to, rather than accommodation with, the oppressor: contemporary readers of the story of the burning fiery furnace would have little difficulty in discerning its message for them. Apocalyptic literature, and above all the Revelation of John which ends the New Testament (and which was written for Christians experiencing Roman persecution), is always both future-oriented and heaven-oriented, and liberally studded with esoteric visions or portents underlining the central message to the oppressed: do not be conformed to this world, do not succumb to easy collaboration, and (above all) do not give up hope: victory, usually accompanied by the wholesale destruction of the oppressors, is certain, even if signs of it are few. From the burning fiery furnace to the experience of twentieth-century black Christians, apocalyptic has remained a powerful and sustaining support for all who are victims of oppression or arbitrary discrimination; and its spirituality is the prayer of protest in its most dramatic and explicit form. It is worth reflecting on what it comprises.

Apocalyptic spirituality is essentially popular, written and articulated *by* rather than simply *for* those about whom it is concerned. It is thus also corporate spirituality: it has to do, not with the personal holiness of the individual but the total salvation of the community, and with the survival of that community's fundamental *raison d'être*. In a century such as ours, with its powerful preoccupation with a narrowly individual approach to life in general, and to religion in particular, this emphasis can provide an important corrective. Apocalyptic spirituality is also fundamentally charismatic, its content often comprising dreams, visions, spiritual ecstasies, heavenly journeys and mysteries,[1] with correspondingly little emphasis on the formal, the cultic, the institutional or the hierarchical. Since visions or prophetic revelations were available to anyone, it is democratic too in inspiration, minimizing the need for sacred ministers or ecclesiastical structures, though with its own traditions and inherited teaching. It was an essential characteristic of the spirituality of early Christians, and an indispensable source of comfort, identity and hope for victims of persecution. With the progressive reduction in importance of the imminent *parousia*, or second coming of Christ, and the eventual recognition and establishment of Christianity in the reign of Constantine, apocalyptic spirituality gradually retreated from the mainstream of Christian life; but with it went some of the Church's lifeblood too. It was in the early monastic communities that the spirituality of the apocalypse retained its significance, as will be seen: the monasteries came increasingly to be seen as representative groups, keeping alive in their prayer and witness and lifestyle something of the charismatic urgency of the spirituality of Revelation, and the sense of persistent struggle against the powers of evil – until even there its cutting edge was insensibly dulled by the steady accretion of liturgical ceremonial or worldly entanglements. Yet it remains an essential, not a marginal, part of both monastic and general Christian spirituality: what is articulated in a particular way in the monastic choir and cell is part of the universal heritage and rhythm of Jewish and Christian lifestyle and experience. And its focus is the prayer of protest, in the sense described in the Introduction (p. 3) – both a challenge to God and a laying-bare of the experience of those who suffer – but this time with two important new features: this is a corporate, not just an individual, spirituality and its protest is directed not just against God but also against the world.

There are a number of distinctive, though closely related, aspects of apocalyptic spirituality which need exploring in turn. The first is its distinctive approach to *time*. Born as it is from the crucible of communal suffering, apocalyptic constantly points towards the future, towards a new age which will be ushered in with the destruction of the oppressor. Heaven was not, as it subsequently became, more or less irrelevant to life on earth, and a kind of twee appendage for the pious or the credulous: rather it was the outright transformation of the unjust earthly order into a new and eternal one, whose values and reality had to be attested to, and *lived*, by all who hoped to inherit it. It is this which lies at the heart of the most famous of all Christian prayers, the 'Our Father': the prayer for God's kingdom to come, and for his will to be done on earth as in heaven, is not empty blathering but an urgent plea for the replacement of the corrupt present age by the new age, the 'other' order of heaven – here, in this world. And the plea not to be led into temptation but to be delivered from evil is in reality a prayer to be kept pure and free from the appalling prospect of damnation at the imminent judgment. As this sense of imminence declined, prayers such as this came to be moralized into general requests for ethical guidance; but their original character belongs to the spirituality of apocalyptic.

The emphasis on the imminence of the new age, and indeed on the fact that the present age is already the 'end-time', recurs frequently in apocalyptic scriptures. The first words of the Book of Revelation express this emphasis perfectly:

A revelation [*apocalupsis*] of Jesus Christ, which God gave him so that he could tell his servants what is now to take place very soon; he sent his angel to make it known to his servant John, and John has borne witness to the Word of God and to the witness of Jesus Christ, everything that he saw. Blessed is anyone who reads the words of this prophecy, and blessed those who hear them, if they treasure the content, because the Time is near. (1:1–3)

Apocalyptic time is radically different from conventional time: instead of being ordered, rhythmic, predictable, it is full of portents, powerfully future-oriented, the seemingly endless months of suffering being seen as nothing when compared with the coming eternity of glory. Above all it is infused with urgency: at any moment this age could be swept away. It is a world-view rich in symbolism and hidden meanings for those with eyes to see them; and the way we live now will powerfully and imminently affect what happens when this end-time is indeed replaced by the new age, the heavenly kingdom.

We may find such an approach naive or irresponsibly alarmist; and there has been no shortage of dubious prophets offering crudely literal interpretations of the books of Daniel or Revelation throughout the Christian centuries. The very urgency which infuses apocalyptic can easily lead to narrow intolerance and unpleasantly self-satisfied élitism, and often has. Yet that offers no excuse for rejecting it outright. At the heart of all apocalyptic writing is a passionate protest against all that encourages people not to worry about the future, or that lulls them into easily assuming either that time is always on our side or that the values of this world are the only ones that matter; and it offers a new and vivid immediacy in our relationship with God. We have to be, as it were, on our toes, alert and watchful for God's word to us in and through the crises and tensions of our own time, seeking not for facile and literalist fulfilments of opaque scriptural prophecies, but rather for guidance in helping to bring about the urgent transformation of our world into the coming kingdom.

It has already been seen that the slow but steady progress of the Christian religion from underground persecution via pluralist tolerance to established recognition inevitably led to a diminution of interest in the 'end-time'. If the new heavenly kingdom was coming it was, it appeared, taking an unconscionably long time over it; and people not unnaturally began to take a greater interest in improving themselves in this world, or seeking growth in uprightness and holiness as though these were ends in themselves, heedless of Christ's repeated warnings about the need for interior repentance and readiness for the coming judgment. In Christian liturgy this emphasis on living in the end-time and eagerly anticipating the coming kingdom of heaven remained alive. In liturgy the future is collapsed into the present, a glimpse of the eternal reality vouchsafed to toiling mortals like struggling mountaineers being afforded a sudden vista of the hitherto mist-shrouded summit. And this is not simply, or even primarily, a hint of what things *might* be like in the next world, but of what things *should* be like in this one. The setting of the *Benedicite* on the lips of Shadrach, Meshach and Abed-Nego in the midst of the burning fiery furnace dramatically testifies to this: this tremendous liturgical song praising the wonders of creation is supremely a prayer of urgent protest, the three men defiantly celebrating the vast God-given glory of this world precisely when they were expected to be leaving it. To sing or pray this canticle today is to make it a part of our own prayer of protest: a determined celebration of the fragile beauty of the world around us while militarized and industrialized societies do everything they can to destroy it. The *Benedicite* is not the sentimental nosegay of the leisured, but the passionate protest of the threatened – the winds and birds and creatures making their own the fragile hope of Nebuchadnezzar's intended victims.

Christian liturgy, then, is an anticipation of the coming new age, and implicitly a challenge to this one. Thomas Merton knew this well:

> The Christian 'present' of the liturgy has something of the character of eternity, in which all reality is present at once ... In every liturgical mystery we have this telescoping of time and eternity, of the universal and the personal, what is common to all ages, what is above and beyond all time and place, and what is most particular and most immediate to our own time and place ... Liturgical time loses its meaning when it becomes simply the complacent celebration of the status quo ... The paradox of liturgical time is that it is humanly insecure, seeking its peace altogether outside the structure of all that is established, visible and familiar, in the hope of a Kingdom which is not seen.[2]

This sense of liturgy as essentially a challenge to contemporary values, embodying a restless and eager anticipation of what is to come, is often lost in much muddled and meandering modern worship. But it retains its character in countless places: in Latin American 'base communities', in the daily prayer of Taize and the charismatic fervour of Pentecostal prayer groups, or wherever groups of Christians meet to sustain each other in stress or suffering or doubt. Such prayer is protest, not only because it challenges the perennial temptations of complacency and apathy but also because it bears witness to the values and vision of a new age. What has sustained the Church in previous centuries is precisely what sustains it now: those myriad clusters of obscure and improbable servants of Christ, breaking bread and lighting candles in draughty churches and high-rise tower blocks, at once waiting for and incarnating the coming kingdom.

It is this emphasis upon *waiting* that is the second primary characteristic of apocalyptic spirituality. Habakkuk, one of the prophets of Israel's exile, articulates in his prayer the cry of his people for deliverance; and the answer he receives is distinctly ambivalent:

> I shall stand at my post,
> I shall station myself on my watch-tower,
> watching to see what he will say to me,
> what answer he will make to my complaints.
> Then Yahweh answered me and said,
> 'Write the vision down,
> inscribe it on tablets
> to be easily read.
> For the vision is for its appointed time,
> it hastens towards its end and it will not lie;
> although it may take some time, wait for it,
> for come it certainly will before too long.' (Hab. 2:1–3)

God will hear and answer his people's cry; but you may have to wait first. The experience of waiting is central to the life of the poor and oppressed, now as then – indeed now even more than then. The rich with their status, credit cards and private transport, do not have to wait for anything; and busy people, accustomed to get what they want when they want it,

are apt to make bad patients in hospitals and holidaymakers
afflicted by aircraft delays. The poor, accustomed to queue
for everything from buses to houses, know only too well what
it means to wait. Paul Harrison records the painfully eloquent
recollection of one of millions in the inner city:

> . . . the worst thing is social security. You sit there for three
> hours waiting, and when you get to see them they talk to
> you as if they're not interested in anything you've got to
> say, as if they don't want to be doing the job. You can
> make an appointment by phone, but you just try getting
> through to them. I spent £1.50 once in a call box. The
> switchboard lady kept saying 'Sorry to keep you waiting',
> and when I finally got through it took just four seconds.
> My giro is due on Thursdays, but sometimes it doesn't
> come till Saturday, then you're right up the creek. I went
> up there one day, waited my three hours, and saw this
> geezer. He said if it's not come tomorrow come back and
> I'll give you a form. I said why wait till tomorrow and
> make me queue three hours again, give me the form now.
> He said that's not our procedure. When I complained, he
> went and checked it with the supervisor. I asked him to let
> me see the supervisor. He said, 'I'm sorry he's busy.' I
> said, 'How can he be, you've just left him.' He said, 'He's
> got someone else with him now.' I said, 'OK, I'll wait till
> he's free.' He said, 'He'll be busy all afternoon.' It's always
> like that.[3]

The experience of waiting recurs throughout the Bible. The
Book of Daniel praises the person who waits (for the mysteriously specific amount of time prescribed, Dan. 12:12); and
the long and gentle Psalm 37 counsels a victim of injustice to
wait patiently for vindication: it was this counsel which was
introduced into Jesus' Beatitudes as part of the Sermon on
the Mount.[4] St Luke describes Simeon, in the exquisite
Candlemas story, waiting for the consolation of Israel and
taking the infant Jesus in his arms in the temple: the old man,
hanging around patiently for reasons that most others would
have found ludicrous or blasphemous or both, is in the end

the one who recognizes Israel's hope in a helpless child; and his little song of thanks as he leaves the stage, overcome with joy and gratitude, is one of scripture's proudest moments: 'Lord, now lettest thou thy servant depart in peace . . . for *mine* eyes have seen thy salvation.'⁵ Later Jesus reminds his hearers of the overriding importance of waiting: 'See that you have your belts done up and your lamps lit. Be like people waiting for their master to return from the wedding feast, ready to open the door as soon as he comes and knocks. Blessed those servants whom the master finds awake when he comes' (Luke 12:36–37). In the Book of Revelation the end of the long period of waiting is at last signalled:

> Then the angel that I had seen, standing on the sea and the land, raised his right hand to heaven, and swore by him who lives for ever and ever . . . The time of waiting is over; at the time when the seventh angel is heard sounding his trumpet, the mystery of God will be fulfilled, just as he announced in the gospel to his servants the prophets.' (Rev. 10:5–7)

In the context, then, of apocalyptic, the experience of apparently hopeless and endless waiting acquires an undergirding of protest and stubborn, strong expectation. In Christian spirituality this is supremely exemplified in the season and liturgy of Advent, as Maria Boulding points out in an important book on this subject.⁶ The Advent themes are above all concerned with this anticipatory, hopeful waiting, for the coming of God – both at Bethlehem as a child, and at the end of the world as judge. This is the expectant waiting of a mother in pregnancy, a common biblical image;⁷ and it offers hope and sustenance to all whose waiting for justice or deliverance is devoid of both.

Yet such waiting is desperately hard, for the poor because it is so often interminable, and for the rich because it is almost always intolerable. We live in an implacably impatient society, where the patient capacity to wait for something has become only the enforced predicament of the deprived, rather than an integral dimension of all human living. Those close to the rhythms of nature know better, and we might profitably learn from them. No amount of technology can in the end produce the spring. You have to wait for it; and sometimes the same is true for us: the readiness to wait, to prepare carefully and attentively, to be still and seek signs of the advent of what we seek, is a central dimension of the Christian life. The majestic Psalm 106 recalls the reckless activism of the Israelites after the crossing of the Red Sea:

> The waters covered their oppressors;
>> not one of them was left alive.
> Then they believed in his words:
> then they sang his praises.
> But they soon forgot his deeds
> and would not wait upon his will.
> They yielded to their cravings in the desert
>> and put God to the test in the wilderness.
> (Ps. 106:11–14 Grail)

Nevertheless this waiting is, even at best, an uncomfortable, even traumatic, experience, shot through with fiercely urgent protest: when, Lord? How long? Why not now? Where are you? The heart of such spirituality for Christians is, as we have already seen, Christ in Gethsemane; and W. H. Vanstone's powerful study has emphasized its importance:[8] St Mark depicts beneath the serene surface of those final words (Mark 14:36) a fearful struggle with doubt and terror as Jesus waits to be handed over, in appalled anticipation of what is to come. Yet that is how all of us stand before God in times of extremity, and our prayer too is likely to be an urgent mixture of protest and hope. In early 1945 a Jesuit priest called Alfred Delp was sentenced to death for complicity in the abortive attempt on Hitler's life. After his final appeal had failed, he wrote:

> What is God's purpose in all this? . . . Does he want us to drain the chalice to the dregs and are these hours of waiting preparation for an extraordinary Advent? Or is he testing our faith? What should I do to remain loyal – go on hoping

despite the hopelessness of it all? Or should I relax? Ought I to resign myself to the inevitable and is it cowardice not to do this and to go on hoping? Should I simply stand still, free and ready to take whatever God sends? I can't yet see the way clear before me ... Often I just sit before God looking at him questioningly.[9]

He records no answer. Yet before they came for him he records, in a final reflection, something very close to what is told of the figure in Gethsemane a thousand years before: 'I will honestly and patiently await God's will. I will trust him till they come to fetch me. I will do my best to ensure that this blessing, too, shall not find me broken and in despair.' Alfred Delp was shot on the feast of Candlemas 1945; but his little *Nunc Dimittis* is as moving and eloquent a testimony as Simeon's to the fitful and fragile glimpses of God in the extremities of human experience.

This in turn introduces the most important aspect of all. There would be no prayer of protest if there were no *hope* in ultimate vindication. But how is this to be distinguished from facile optimism? The spirituality of apocalyptic has two answers: first, in the light of its distinctive view of time, it seeks to bring something of the future into the present, and to celebrate now the fulfilment of what is hoped for *even before it is achieved*. The momentous twelfth chapter of Revelation witnesses a sudden shift from predictions of what is to come to celebrations in advance, as it were, of victory. Is this mere wishful thinking? It depends on your perspective; Allan Boesak has this to say about the chapter:

And now again there is a song of praise. Many make the mistake of interpreting this song as they do the other songs in this book, in a purely triumphalistic fashion. Others ask if it is not premature to sing when the battle is not yet over. Neither view is correct. Oppressed people in South Africa understand the need for singing. Sometimes a song is a song of triumph, celebrating a success, expressing hope that the ultimate victory will come. It is a song of anticipation ... Such a song is the song of Revelation 12.

73

This song has nothing to do with the shallow, triumphalistic 'Jesus-is-the-answer' theology with which oppressed people are so often taught to comfort themselves. Neither is it premature, for the battle is won, even though the struggle is not yet over. And besides, it drives the dragon crazy when you sing about his downfall even though you are bleeding.[10]

This is why the author of the Book of Daniel sets the *Benedicite* on the lips of the three men even before the outcome is established. Apocalyptic hope is an outrageous challenge to present reality; and like Shadrach, Meshach and Abed-Nego we are called to drive our Nebuchadnezzars crazy by celebrating victory in the very heart of defeat. To hear psalms of thanksgiving echoing from the depths of the gas chambers, or the early Christian *Te Deum laudamus* from those facing certain and bloody martyrdom, is to encounter hope in its most furiously paradoxical form, for to give thanks as you die defeated appears in worldly terms the most tragic of delusions. But in apocalyptic terms it is the future collapsed into the present, the powerful destroyed at the moment of victory by the supervention of a radically new perspective, Shadrach the martyr's prayer of protest drowning the thunder of Nebuchadnezzar the king's bagpipes and horns.

Secondly apocalyptic hope carries within it an almost incommunicable secret, perhaps known only to those who have experienced it: a sense, however dimly felt and affirmed, of God's intimate and sustaining presence in the midst of their despair and suffering. In his book *AIDS: sharing the pain*, Bill Kirkpatrick quotes Fr Bernard Lynch's answer to the question of how we might show compassion to all who suffer:

It happens by people like you and me reaching out to one another, not with judgment but with an openness that is love. To be open to someone is to become that person; a person becomes what they are open to. For us to be open as Christians is to be open to the infinite possibilities of an infinitely loving God. Literally the skies are the limit. We are called not into a spirit of slavery but into a spirit of freedom.[11]

So to protest, and to hope, is in some sense to discover, *in the very act of protesting*, the reality of God's love already at work within you. We have seen this strange phenomenon in the story of Job; and it is reflected also in the burning fiery furnace, where the three walk free in the flames with a mysterious fourth figure, 'like a child of the gods', in there with them. The idea will occur again in later chapters: it must be sufficient now to illustrate it with a final example.

When I visited Namibia in 1980 I went to see a very old woman whose son was then serving a long prison sentence for being a founder member of SWAPO. She lived in the black township, in a tiny corrugated-iron hut; and she was almost blind. Yet she radiated not just quiet conviction that her son and her country would one day be free, but also an extraordinary sense of some deeper love that held her upright and kept her company. I suddenly thought as I sat there: this person is not just aware of God's love. She's on fire with it. When, a few years later, her son was indeed set free it was only the setting of a seal on a triumph that was, in some strange sense, already hers. As with Shadrach, Meshach and Abed-Nego, the real miracle was not the ultimate victory but the gentle yet indestructible hope; and once again Nebuchadnezzar was to find that the game was lost even before the furnace was kindled. What sustained adherents of apocalyptic was not a courageous conviction that they would one day win through, but an extraordinary discovery that in some mysterious sense they had done so already; not just a general hope in God's justice but also a personal glimpse of God's *presence*.

What does all this have to say to us? We have already seen that the sense of urgency, and of living in the 'end-time', gradually disappeared from Christianity as its own position in society steadily improved. But there was another reason as well. Apocalyptic spirituality gave people a powerful identity and cohesion, but at a price: they had to separate themselves entirely from any hint of conformity with society around them; and they had to mark that separation by observing moral and religious precepts of exceptional severity. The same was true of the Jews: when they were dispersed throughout the world after the destruction of Jerusalem by the Romans, their ritual, moral precepts and religious practices acquired a new importance in preserving their cultural and communal integrity in the face of constant temptations to conform to the society around them.[12] All apocalyptic literature reserves its most furious condemnation for those who accommodate themselves; and the first three chapters of the Book of Revelation illustrate this vividly, as John of Patmos berates individual churches for allowing the cutting-edge of their religious faith and practice to be subtly softened.

Yet they also illustrate something else. Apocalyptic literature is not simply a revealing of the truth about the future, in this world or the next. It is also a revealing of the truth about the present, and not just in heaven but here and now. John of Patmos does not just lay bare for his readers what vision of triumph God has in store for them: he also lays bare what is wrong wth the way they are living now. The final ingredient of apocalyptic spirituality is its overriding demand for a *response* from those to whom it is directed; and that, in the end, includes us all. The medieval wall-paintings and mystery plays depicting doomsday express this with graphic ferocity: we are all under judgment, all living under the shadow of apocalypse, *sub specie aeternitatis*. The ferocious words of the medieval *Dies Irae*, which became part of the liturgy of requiem masses and the subject of incandescent musical settings by Verdi, Berlioz and others, express this powerfully:

> *Quid sum miser tunc dicturus?*
> *Quem patronum rogaturus,*
> *Cum vix justus sit securus?*

> What shall I, frail man, be pleading?
> Who for me be interceding?
> When the just are mercy needing?[13]

We might go further: if I do not speak out for those who are the current victims of popular hatred or social taboo, who will there be to speak out for me?

The form that such a response will take must inevitably vary with the circumstances. For some, like Shadrach, Meshach and Abed-Nego, or Father Alfred Delp, it will be one of quiet but enormous courage which is all the greater precisely because it is grounded in deeply human doubt and uncertainty. For others, like Christ in Gethsemane or the old woman in Namibia, it may be no more and no less than the capacity to watch and wait, and perhaps to help one another in fostering a creative and expectant, hope-filled waiting that transmutes the grinding destructiveness of the experience of so many. For others it may require a shared willingness, like Allan Boesak and the Book of Revelation, to celebrate ultimate victory even before it appears remotely in sight, and thereby directly to assist in its achievement. For many it will present a temptation to which adherents of apocalyptic have sometimes succumbed – the temptation to take refuge in intolerant and even fanatical sectarianism that can be little better than the injustice it opposes. But for everyone it will demand a searching self-exploration in the light of an urgent and overriding question: how can I bear witness to the values of God's coming kingdom even when (in fact precisely when) it is far from clear that they will ever be fashionable, let alone triumphant? In making our own response to that question we may, like millions before us, want to protest vehemently against a God so apparently slow to usher in that kingdom, so seemingly blind when his children falter or fail. But we may also find, like many of those millions, that even in the very act of protesting a shadowy figure 'like a child of the gods' is at our side, and Nebuchadnezzar's band has suddenly fallen silent.

NOTES

1   See, e.g., 2 Cor. 12; or Rev. 2.
2   Thomas Merton, *Time and the Liturgy* (1955), repr. in *Meditations on Liturgy*. London, Mowbrays, 1976.

3 Paul Harrison, *Inside the Inner City* (London, Penguin, 1983), p. 117.
4 Psalm 37, esp. vv. 7–9; cf. Matt. 5:1–12, esp. v. 4.
5 The *Nunc Dimittis*, Luke 2: 29–30.
6 *The Coming of God*. London, SPCK, 1982.
7 See, e.g., Rom. 8:19; John 16:21; Rev. 12.
8 W. H. Vanstone, *The Stature of Waiting*. London, DLT, 1982.
9 *Facing death: prison meditations of Alfred Delp* (London, Bloomsbury, 1962), pp. 187–91 passim.
10 Allan Boesak, *Comfort and Protest: reflections on the apocalypse of John of Patmos* (St Andrew's Press, 1987), p. 87.
11 Bill Kirkpatrick, *AIDS: sharing the pain* (London, DLT, 1988), p. 101.
12 Christopher Rowland, *Radical Christianity* (Cambridge, Polity Press, 1988), p. 47.
13 English tr. from the English Hymnal. Oxford University Press, 1933.

FURTHER READING

Allan Boesak, *Comfort and Protest: Reflections on the Apocalypse of John of Patmos*. St Andrew's Press, 1987.

Bernard McGinn (ed.), *Apocalyptic Spirituality*. Classics of Western Spirituality. London, SPCK, 1979.

W. H. Vanstone, *The Stature of Waiting*. London, DLT, 1982.

Norman Cohn, *The Pursuit of the Millennium*. London, Temple Smith, 1970.

E. S. Fiorenza, *The Book of Revelation: justice and judgment*. Philadelphia, Fortress Press, 1985.

Christopher Rowland, *The Open Heaven: a study of apocalyptic in Judaism and early Christianity*. London, SPCK, 1982.

Christopher Rowland, *Radical Christianity*. Cambridge, Polity Press, 1988.

5

The Call of the Wilderness
The Desert Tradition

In our exploration thus far of some of the themes of biblical spirituality, one distinctive and important aspect has been left untouched. Jacob and Moses, Jeremiah and even Jesus did not simply struggle with God in a vacuum: they did it on their own, in the desert or wilderness, not because they were concerned only with themselves but because it was there that God made himself known to them. The call of the wilderness has exerted a constant influence on subsequent spirituality, and never more powerfully than in our own century. We might then begin our exploration of its importance there.

On the evening of 1 December 1916, in the remote Saharan settlement of Tamanrasset, a French ex-playboy and soldier called Charles de Foucauld was murdered by a group of Senoussi tribesmen. It was a tragic, even bizarre, end to an extraordinary life: like Augustine before him and Thomas Merton after him, de Foucauld appears to have felt the need to atone for an earlier existence of carnal indulgence by withdrawing to a desert life of the most extreme asceticism; and, again like Augustine and Merton, this dramatic conversion has had an immense influence on subsequent generations. All three were passionate and dynamic people; and each brought the same restless energy to his asceticism as he had once brought to the sparkling social scene in Milan, Sant-Cyr or Cambridge. De Foucauld was not the first, nor the most extraordinary, of those who sought God in the desert; but he exemplifies in a particularly vivid way both the allure and the strangeness, both the high romance and the extreme cost, of desert spirituality. Above all though, he personifies its exotic foreignness: the whole enterprise seems aeons away from the life and experience of ordinary people, and no more relevant to our lives than Cinderella or James Bond.

It was not always so, however. In the story of the Exodus the desert had been both a symbol and a setting for Israel's most costly encounters with God. In the long journey from Egypt to the Promised Land, as was seen in Chapter 1, Moses has to cope with the impatience and complaints of his people; and his relationship with God is marked by the rapid alternations of affection, reverence and furious protest that might be expected to characterize so intimate a friendship. God fed his people with manna for forty years (Exod. 16:35); and, perhaps not surprisingly, the Israelites finally grew tired of it, nostalgically hankering for lost gourmet delights. The Authorized Version beautifully captures their feelings: 'We remember the fish, which we did eat in Egypt freely; the cucumbers, and the melons, and the leeks, and the onions, and the garlick; But now our soul is dried away: there is nothing at all, beside this manna, before our eyes' (Num. 11:5–6). Moses rounds on God with all the anger and protest of an overwrought leader unfairly blamed for a nation's ills:

'Why do you treat your servant so badly? In what respect have I failed to win your favour, for you to lay the burden of all these people on me? Was it I who conceived all these people, was I their father, for you to say to me, "Carry them in your arms, like a foster-father carrying an unweaned child, to the country which I swore to give their fathers"? Where am I to find meat to give all these people, pestering me with their tears and saying, "Give us meat to eat"? I cannot carry all these people on my own; the weight is too much for me. If this is how you mean to treat me, please kill me outright!' (Num. 11:11–15)

God hears his cry and arranges for some of the elders to share his burden.

Later, and more famous still, the prophet Elijah, exhausted by his endless struggles with Ahab and Jezebel, retreats alone to the desert and pours out his heart to God:

He came to Beersheba, a town of Judah, where he left his servant. He himself went on into the desert, a day's journey, and sitting under a furze bush wished he were dead. 'Yahweh,' he said, 'I have had enough. Take my life; I am no better than my ancestors.' (1 Kgs 19:4)

Again, however, the Lord responds; and the narrative of their encounter on the mountainside is a crucial moment both in the Bible and in the spirituality of the desert. But it is worth remembering that the famous appearance of the Lord in 'a still small voice' (1 Kgs 19:12 AV) is not a source of personal comfort but the transmission of a terrible command, ordering Elijah to return and anoint a new king who will destroy the worshippers of Baal; and it is also worth emphasizing that God appeared to Elijah, not in a moment of serene solitary contemplation but in response to the prophet's desperate cry for help. Those who fled to the desert, like Jesus during his temptations, found themselves in a place where their deepest wounds and weaknesses were sharply exposed; but they also found their prayers of protest answered, even if not always in the way they might have wished. And these prayers were never only, or even primarily, for themselves: they were for those from whom they had fled and to whom they must return.[1]

In the early centuries of the Christian Church ordinary men and women in their thousands sought God in the desert; and their ferociously ascetic lifestyle won them as much opprobrium as praise. The lofty philippic of Edward Gibbon, in the course of his famous onslaught on monasticism in Chapter 37 of the *Decline and Fall*, is worth quoting:

The monks were divided into two classes: the *Coenobites*, who lived under a common and regular discipline; and the *Anachorets*, who indulged their unsocial, independent fanaticism. The most devout, or the most ambitious, of the spiritual brethren renounced the convent, as they had renounced the world. The fervent monasteries of Egypt, Palestine, and Syria were surrounded by a *Laura*, a distant circle of solitary cells; and the extravagant penance of the

Hermits was stimulated by applause and emulation . . . This voluntary martyrdom must have gradually destroyed the sensibility both of the mind and body; nor can it be presumed that the fanatics who torment themselves are susceptible of any lively affection for the rest of mankind . . . But the golden legend of their lives was embellished by the artful credulity of their interested brethren; and a believing age was easly persuaded that the slightest caprice of an Egyptian or a Syrian monk had been sufficient to interrupt the eternal laws of the universe. The favourites of Heaven were accustomed to cure inveterate diseases with a touch, a word, or a distant message; and to expel the most obstinate demons from the souls or bodies which they possessed. They familiarly accosted, or imperiously commanded, the lions and serpents of the desert; infused vegetation into a sapless trunk; suspended iron on the surface of the water; passed the Nile on the back of a crocodile; and refreshed themselves in a fiery furnace.[2]

Gibbon's Olympian rationalism is of course the extreme antithesis of the spirituality of the desert, even if he does legitimately draw attention to the fundamental *strangeness* of the people who, like de Foucauld, went to live there; and he rightly lampoons the dubious mystique which often surrounded them. He is cruelly unfair however in implying that they went there to draw attention to themselves, or that their asceticism was indulged in simply for its own sake. In his Life of St Antony, the founder of monasticism, St Athanasius makes it clear that he went there not only to seek God, but also to challenge and confront the powers of evil that threatened humanity. This was not just a flight *from* the world, then, but also a flight *for* it; and Antony's prayer was invariably an active and costly engagement, not an idle or disengaged contemplation: '[The brothers] also observed him struggling as if against things visible, and praying against them; and . . . at the same time he fought, kneeling and praying to the Lord.'[3] Earlier, and after a particularly gruelling struggle wth the devil, Antony, like Moses, turns on God for not supporting him sooner:

In this circumstance also the Lord did not forget the wrestling of Antony, but came to his aid ... Suddenly the demons vanished from view, [and] the pain of his body ceased instantly ... Aware of the assistance and both breathing more easily and relieved from the sufferings, Antony entreated the vision that appeared, saying, 'Where were you? Why didn't you appear in the beginning, so that you could stop my distresses?'[4]

Many who, freely or involuntarily, have found themselves alone in the desert, either literally or through bereavement or deprivation or tragedy, will have echoed St Antony's prayer of protest; and not all will have prevailed as he did over the powers of evil. For them, as for Antony and Moses and Elijah, the desert is not just a place where illusions are stripped and harsh realities uncomfortably apprehended. It is first and foremost a place of death; and people who find themselves there are likely not only to protest against evil but also to protest against God.

And it is only when seen in this light that the spirituality of the desert even begins to make sense. For as long as it is understood simply as some kind of creative testing-ground, a form of divine assault-course designed to produce a holy élite, it will have nothing whatever to say to the experience of the millions who live 'in the desert' without any choice in the matter; and it will deserve all the patrician invective of which Gibbon and others are capable. But once it becomes clear that people went to the desert, not just to assuage their guilt feelings or to develop their spiritual muscles, but to challenge all the evil and gross unfairness that the world throws at them, and to engage with the God who created it all, the spirituality of the desert begins to come alive. People went there to face death, not so that the rest of us will not have to, but precisely in order to give us courage to do the same, in whatever deserts of human experience we find ourselves. Yet there is a more important point still, and one which for Christians is the heart of the matter. It is made clear in one of the sayings of the early desert fathers:

A brother asked an old man, 'How can I be saved?' The latter took off his habit, girded his loins and raised his hands to heaven, saying, 'So should the monk be: denuded of all things in this world, and crucified . . . his arms outstretched in the form of a cross to heaven, calling on God.'[5]

Those who went freely to the desert to experience and share the suffering and poverty that millions endure without choice did so for one overriding reason: because God went there first. And if, however mixed their motives, their apparently useless self-sacrifice could be united with Christ's and in some sense be made redemptive, as they believed his to have been, then their prayer in the desert might not only change their lives: it might also change the world.

It is this above all which animated the desert people, from Antony to Charles de Foucauld and beyond. De Foucauld, like the early desert fathers, saw prayer not as a technique to be employed and fine-tuned, but as a *life* to be embarked upon in direct imitation of Christ, sharing the poverty and homelessness and insecurity that were once his. Like St Augustine centuries earlier, de Foucauld did not simply forget his colourful past: he allowed it to become the raw material for a new present and future: 'I am an old sinner,' he wrote in 1905, 'who, after his conversion nearly twenty years ago, was given a powerful attraction by Jesus to lead the life he led at Nazareth.'[6] The reference to Nazareth is important, and not only because de Foucauld spent time in Palestine: he sought to identify with the hidden life of Christ, in the barren and unvarying routine that he supposed Christ to have experienced at Nazareth. And this imitation of Christ was never intended as mere posturing, or pious observance for its own sake: 'I must go where souls have the greatest need,' he wrote in 1901, 'not to the holiest place';[7] and he went to the Sahara not because it was the loneliest place in the world but because it was the poorest, and thus the place where Christ was to be both encountered and incarnated. It was not just his Catholic background and disposition that led de Foucauld to a particularly vivid sense of Christ's presence, both in the eucharistic bread and in the lives of the poor; and it was this above all which the Little Brothers and Sisters of Jesus, whose rule is based upon his life and teaching, seek to emphasize. René Voillaume, the order's founder, wrote eloquently about this presence:

> For us, as for the generations before us, the sign of the eucharist is that of the calm and unchanging appearance of the bread and wine. But the reality to which this spiritual nourishment and this mystical offering are due, sprang from the anguish of a human heart, a sweat-drenched face, a body shuddering as it was racked by pain, wounds from which the blood dripped and the long drawn-out agony of a criminal's death. All this was borne for us by God. Without this torment of the Passion there would be no sacrament ... If participation in the eucharist fails to move us to welcome all suffering as our share in that which counted most for Jesus, and still more, to seek out sacrifice, then our participation in it is barren.[8]

So the vocation of de Foucauld and those who followed his inspiration was to a particular kind of presence, a silent loving identification with the poor at whatever cost; and the real presence of Christ in the eucharistic bread both symbolizes and sustains those who seek to make him present in their own lives – without condition, without expecting a response, without even speaking. The Little Brothers and Sisters of Jesus still seek to do that, not just in the literal desert of the Sahara but in the equally barren deserts of decaying inner-city estates.

And this is the very reverse of the élitist spiritual athleticism which Gibbon justly excoriated. Voillaume points out that 'Our Lord even inserted *contradiction* and not unity into our lives, the moment he became part of them';[9] and the contradiction to which he refers is the dichotomy of flesh and spirit, of dust and breath, which marked human beings from the beginning of time (cf. Gen. 2:4–7). So to be in union with Christ is to make your own this basic contradiction, and to live it out, which in turn means that prayer becomes an honest bearing of that contradiction, not an escape from it:

The vocation of the Petits-Frères, more than any other, puts us at the heart of the contradiction in the world, at its storm centre, because we are deposited on the spot where an attempt is being made to implant the contemplation of the invisible and crucified God in the daily life of mankind.[10]

In prayer the Little Brothers and Sisters struggle to hold together both the unconditional love they owe to God, and the anxieties and suffering of those among whom they live; and this in turn gives their prayer a quality of restless dissatisfaction, even of frustration: the brothers and sisters sit in silence before the sacrament, not with the easy leisure of the privileged but with the weary resoluteness of the poor who have to go on with the relentless round of daily life whether they want to or not. And their prayer will be 'like an appeal shouted to God'[11] in exactly the same way as Elijah's was, both for themselves and for everyone like them: Voillaume asks himself where God is in the vast poverty of India;[12] and Carlo Carretto, another of the Little Brothers, underlines this sense of solidarity with all who suffer:

> If I love, if I really love, how can I tolerate the fact that a third of humanity is menaced with starvation while I enjoy the security of economic stability? If I act in that way I shall perhaps be a good Christian, but I shall certainly not be a saint; and today there are far too many good Christians when the world needs saints. We must learn to accept instability, put ourselves every now and then in the condition of having to say, 'Give us this day our daily bread,' with real anxiety because the larder is empty; have the courage, for love of God and one's neighbour, to give until it hurts and, above all, keep open in the wall of the soul the great window of living faith in the Providence of an all-powerful God.[13]

So the heart of desert spirituality is this concern to make Christ present in the midst of death and deprivation, and to make explicit in prayer the contradiction of a crucified God.

John Cassian, the fourth-century monk whose 'Conferences' contains the essence of this spirituality, says that the purest prayer is not verbal at all, but the pouring-forth to God of our deepest feelings 'with groanings and sighs that cannot be uttered';[14] and in his last letter, written hours before he died, de Foucauld tells his friend that:

> Your sufferings, your past and new anxieties which you have accepted and offered to God in union with the sufferings of Jesus, are not only the sole things, but the most precious that God gives you in order that you may come before him with your hands full . . . One knows that one does not love enough, and it is true that one does not ever love enough, but God who knows from what clay he has made us, and who loves us more than any mother can love her child, has said, 'He who dieth not will not reject him that cometh to him.'[15]

The desert people will always be odd, redundant, perverse folk on the margins of conventional society, even when they live in the heart of urban ghettos and tower blocks. Sister Benedicta Ward memorably encapsulates their character: 'They are men who recognise . . . that they are broken, incomplete, and they learn to remain incomplete, with their raw edges reaching always towards the heavens.'[16] Such people will doubtless always be few; and few even of them will have the aura of a de Foucauld. It is easy to exaggerate their qualities, and important from time to time to question their *raison d'être*: there have certainly been times when the spirituality of the desert seems to reflect more of a naive or manipulative egotism than a genuine concern for others. And yet such people do no more than to make explicit, in the starkest possible way, what all of us must confront some of the time, and some of us all of the time: the reality of death, the nature of evil and of undeserved suffering, as well as the implications for everyone of a world where millions, if they pray at all, must make their own the terrible despairing cry of the exhausted Elijah. It will always be easy to deride the fierce asceticism of Antony or de Foucauld: too easy, perhaps, until our prayer like theirs becomes an active identification with the poor among whom they lived and died.

There is however a final point to be made, a further contradiction about the spirituality of the desert which takes us back to the story of Moses and Israel at Sinai. For them the desert was not just a place where God caused them to suffer: it was also where he established an entirely new and intimate relationship with them, in the covenant that gave Jewish spirituality its distinctive character and hope. Even when the Israelites again and again broke the covenant, God constantly re-established it with the forgiving and enduring love of a husband for his unfaithful wife: he protests at human faithlessness but in the end promises a reconciliation that will transform even the desert, in a marvellous passage in the Book of Hosea:

> Therefore, behold, I will allure her, and bring her into the wilderness, and speak comfortably unto her. And I will give her her vineyards from thence, and the valley of Achor for a door of hope; and she shall sing there, as in the days of her youth, and as in the day when she came up out of the land of Egypt ... And in that day will I make a covenant for them with the beasts of the field, and with the fowls of heaven, and with the creeping things of the ground; and I will break the bow and the sword and the battle out of the earth, and will make them to lie down safely. And I will betroth thee unto me for ever; yea, I will betroth thee unto me in righteousness, and in judgment, and in lovingkindness, and in mercies ... and I will have mercy upon her that had not obtained mercy; and I will say to them which were not my people, Thou art my people; and they shall say, Thou art my God. (Hos. 2:14–23 AV)

The sacramental presence of Christ in the Sahara, in shelters for the homeless, in church crypts where alcoholics spend Christmas and in soulless subways where drug addicts spend their life savings, is not just a sign of identification or solidarity: it is a sign of protest and of hope. For the desert, whatever form it takes, is the place where our protest and

God's intersect: our outcry at a Creator who appears to sit idly while his creatures suffer collides with God's plea to his people to repent of their short-sighted self-seeking before it is too late. The desert people who live out the ultimate implications of this collision thereby remind us of the deepest truth to which it points: that if we too had the courage to confront, in prayer and action, the harshest realities of evil and death, and to challenge both the injustice and the inertia that allows them to prevail we might ourselves discover what de Foucauld calls 'the holy liberty of the sons of God,'[17] and a vision of the future that dwarfs our grandest expectations:

> Abba Lot went to see Abba Joseph and said to him, 'Abba, as far as I can I say my little office, I fast a little, I pray and meditate, I live in peace and as far as I can, I purify my thoughts. What else can I do?' Then the old man stood up and stretched his hands towards heaven. His fingers became like ten lamps of fire and he said to him, 'If you will, you can become all flame.'[18]

NOTES

1 Dorothée Soelle, writing about this passage, says 'Elijah now begins the return journey into the world. The prophet's political mission is renewed; he does not bow down in worship, nor does he found a monastery on the site of his blessed experience. Instead, he finds the way back into and for the world', *The Inward Road*, tr. Scheidt (London, DLT, 1979), p. 68.
2 Gibbon, *The Decline and Fall of the Roman Empire* (London, Everyman's Library), vol. IV, ch. 37, pp. 16–19.
3 St Athanasius, 'The Life of Antony', tr. Gregg in Classics of Western Spirituality (London, SPCK, 1980), p. 70.
4 ibid. p. 39.
5 *The Wisdom of the Desert Fathers*, tr. Benedicta Ward (Oxford, SLG Press, 1979), p. 3.
6 Charles de Foucauld, *Meditations of a Hermit*, tr. Balfour (London, Burns & Oates, 1981), pp. 155–6.
7 ibid. p. 158.
8 René Voillaume, *Brothers of Men: letters to the Petits Frères* (London, DLT, 1966, repr. 1972), p. 44.

9 ibid. p. 209.
10 ibid. p. 210.
11 ibid. p. 98.
12 ibid. p. 199
13 Carlo Carretto, *Letters from the Desert*, tr. Hancock (London, DLT, 1972), pp. 80–1.
14 Cassian, 'Conferences' 10.11, tr. Chadwick in Western Asceticism, vol. X in Library of Christian Classics (Philadelphia, 1958), p. 244.
15 de Foucauld, op. cit. p. 184.
16 *The Lives of the Desert Fathers*, introd. Benedicta Ward SLG (London, Mowbrays, 1981), p. 34.
17 de Foucauld, op. cit. p. 93.
18 *The Sayings of the Desert Fathers*, tr. Benedicta Ward SLG (London, Mowbrays, 1981), p. 103.

FURTHER READING

Derwas Chitty, *The Desert a City*. Oxford, Blackwell, 1966.
The Lives of the Desert Fathers, tr. Benedicta Ward. London, Mowbrays, 1981.
The Sayings of the Desert Fathers, tr. Benedicta Ward. London, Mowbrays, 1981.
Charles de Foucauld, *Meditations of a Hermit*, tr. Balfour. London, Burns & Oates, 1981.
René Voillaume, *Seeds of the Desert*. London, Burns & Oates, 1955.
René Voillaume, *Brothers of Men*. London, DLT, 1971.
Carlo Carretto, *Letters from the Desert*. London, DLT, 1972.

6

The Child's Question
Julian of Norwich

Among the various memories that occasionally rise like phantoms to torment me in the darker watches of the night is that of an infants' school assembly I once had to take. A young and inexperienced curate at the time, I prepared with the utmost care. I had a story to tell, rehearsed a dozen times before a mirror, until every possible misleading word or unhelpful complication had been excised and nothing left to chance. It was, if I remember rightly, a happy little tale about bunnies, which I felt would go down well at harvest festival time. I duly appeared before the hushed throng and told my story. It seemed to be well received. They remained hushed (always a good sign). I sat down, perspiring and exhausted. At once a little boy raised his hand and stared at me piercingly. 'Sir,' he asked, 'why did Jesus have to die?' I sagged despairingly, and stumbled to my feet.

The capacity of little children to ask the most difficult of all questions at the most awkward possible moment is proverbial. What is less often noticed is that those who manage to retain a childlike sense of wonder and joy about the world around them often exhibit the same capacity. Contemplation, whether of the beauties of nature or of God, is not the untroubled and placid affair it is commonly supposed to be; and those who, in art or music or religion, probe most deeply into the mysteries of the universe often seem to combine visions of transcendental grandeur with the most searching questions about the meaning of it all. When Jesus invited people to become like little children if they wanted to enter the kingdom of heaven, we naturally suppose him to have had in mind a child's capacity for trust and love. But he may also have had in mind a child's propensity for asking the most diifficult questions. As a child, presumably, he asked them himself.

Few figures in the Christian spiritual tradition exhibit this childlike readiness both to trust and to question, to contemplate and to protest, as much as Julian of Norwich. Although her 'Revelations of the Divine Love' begins with, and is grounded in, the exploration of God's love for us, rather than of our love for God, it derives directly from her own experience – not only of suffering but also of bafflement. She wanted to know why a God of love could possibly permit, let alone create, a world full of sin and evil. So she asked him. Her insights into God's love are not complementary to, let alone an escape from, her question: rather they are the only credible answer to it. Understood in this context Julian's visions become universal because her question is universal: she asked what all of us must ask, which is why her spirituality is the very opposite of a privatized search for holiness. Indeed this is lay spirituality of the finest possible kind, not only because it was written by a lay woman (in all probability one who had been a mother or widow rather than a nun) but also because it addresses the condition of us all.

Julian is one of the most remarkable and original writers in the Christian tradition; and even now there exists no scholarly consensus about whose works (if any) she had read and which (if any) previous writers had influenced her most. Her terminology, style and approach to traditional theological questions like the nature of God or the problem of evil are genuinely original, and different from those of any who had written before her. This perhaps should not surprise us, and it certainly would not have surprised her: she wrote about what she had been shown by God, not about what she had studied or pondered for herself. It is never easy to assess, let alone to authenticate, the writings of those who claim divine inspiration or revelation as their source, though we may reasonably suspect those who use it to advance a partisan viewpoint or inflate their own egos. It is all the more striking to discover that Julian uses it for neither of these: instead, like the child at school assembly, she absorbs and reflects on what is revealed to her; and then she responds to it. And her response offers us a new insight into the prayer of protest: with Julian of Norwich it takes the form, not of angry complaint against God but of a child's puzzled question to a parent it loves about a world it does not understand. Like a child, Julian perseveres when she does not at once receive an answer that satisfies. And, like a child, her questions are the most simple, and searching, of all.

Julian rarely uses the word 'contemplate' or its cognates in her work: instead, and throughout, she uses the word 'behold' in her descriptions of what was revealed to her. Not surprisingly she frequently has in mind an intimate experience of God: she refers to Mary's 'reverent beholding' of her Lord and maker (LT 4), and later says that we can, through God's grace, 'stand in ghostly beholding' of his endless love (LT 6). Indeed she goes further when she reflects on the Trinity dwelling within the human soul:

> This was a delectable sight and a restful showing, and is so without end. And the beholding of this while we are in this world is very pleasant to God and of very great profit to us. And the soul that thus beholds it becomes like the one it is beholding . . . (LT 68)

Yet this is no rarefied contemplation, cut off from the exigencies of the real world. Immediately after describing with immense power the experience of beholding the suffering Christ (LT 10), Julian writes:

> And after this I saw God in a moment of time, that is to say in my understanding, by which sight I saw that he is in all things. I beheld with much thought, seeing and knowing in sight with a soft dread, and thought: 'What is sin?' for I saw truly that God does everything, however small. And I saw truly that nothing is done by chance or circumstance, but everything by the foreseeing wisdom of God. (LT 11)

The result, then, of Julian's 'beholding' of God is not a

description of the raptures of contemplative ecstasy but a direct confrontation with one of Christianity's greatest difficulties: if God is omnipotent, where do sin and evil come from? The answer she receives, that sin is 'no deed' ('nothing' in the earlier Short Text), is followed by the assurance that further enlightenment is yet to come. Meanwhile Julian continues by beholding the crucified and tortured Christ (LT 12): the juxtaposition of her own question with the vision of the suffering of Jesus is of course not coincidental, and occurs again. In Chapter 15 Julian describes graphically the alternation of 'well-being and woe' in her own life, pointing out that the woe is not always caused by human sin, and insisting that God loves us equally whatever befalls us: again in Chapter 16 she continues with a description of the dying Christ that would do justice to a Grunewald altarpiece.

Before exploring this further it is important to return to Julian's emphasis upon 'beholding'. It is already clear that Julian has in mind something much wider than what is often understood by 'contemplation' or contemplative prayer. It is not only God whom she beholds: she also beholds sin (LT 11), though she warns that beholding other people's sin causes 'as it were a thick mist [to form] before the eye of the soul' (LT 76). She discusses too the value of beholding ourselves:

> for when we begin to hate sin and amend ourselves by the ordinance of holy church, yet there dwells a dread that hinders us, by the beholding of ourselves and of our already-committed sins . . . And the beholding of this makes us so sorry and so heavy that we can hardly find any comfort. (LT 73)

Later she distinguishes between beholding God and beholding self, and points to their essential complementarity:

> And I understood that while we are in this life, it is very profitable for us to see both these things together; for the higher beholding keeps us in spiritual solace and true enjoyment of God; while the other, that is the lower beholding,

keeps us in dread and makes us ashamed of ourselves. (LT 82)

Human beings are, as she puts it, 'a marvellous medley of well-being and woe ... we have in us our risen Lord Jesus and we have in us the wretchedness of the mischief of Adam's fall and dying' (LT 52). In short, we are walking paradoxes, not simply because we are formed out of both earth and heaven, dust and spirit, but because we have within ourselves both Adam and Jesus, both death and resurrection. Hence her emphasis on a God who beholds us, not with lofty detachment but with intense and infinite love:

> Then our good Lord Jesus Christ asked: 'Are you well pleased that I suffered for you?' I said: 'Yes, good Lord, all thanks to you! Yes, good Lord, blessed may you be!' Then Jesus, our kind Lord, said: 'If you are pleased, I am pleased. It is a joy, a bliss, an endless delight to me that ever I suffered my passion for you; and if I could suffer more, I would suffer more.' (LT 22)

Julian 'beholds' this tremendous paradox of a sinful humanity that is none the less infinitely loved: 'and this was a singular marvel and a full and delectable beholding, that we should be [Christ's] crown' (LT 22).

It might by now be clear that Julian's 'beholding' leads her to an integrated and sharply realistic view of humanity, neither excessively affirmative nor unduly fatalistic. It also leads her to a remarkable and original understanding of God, who is at once 'courteous' and 'homely', as she comes to see when reflecting on Mary 'beholding' her dying son on the cross. 'Homeliness', it becomes clear, means something much more profound than our use of the word suggests: God's homeliness is exemplified in the crucified Christ, for thereby he 'makes his home in us' (cf. John 14:23); and later Julian considers its implications:

> Flee to our Lord and we shall be comforted; touch him and we shall be made clean; cleave to him and we shall be sure

95

and safe from all manner of peril; for our courteous Lord
wills that we be as homely with him as heart may think or
soul may desire. But beware that we do not take this
homeliness so recklessly that we leave courtesy [behind];
for our Lord himself is sovereign homeliness, and [yet], he
is as courteous as he is homely. [LT 77]

We are called then, to treat God both as intimate friend and
as a courteous and merciful lord. God is at once 'the highest
and the most mighty, the noblest and the most worthy' and
'the lowest and the most meek, the homeliest and the most
courteous' (LT 7). The centrepiece of her work is the parable
of the lord and the servant (LT 51), in which the servant
runs to do his lord's will but stumbles and falls helpless: the
lord, who represents God the Father, 'beholds' his servant
with intense compassion, or shared suffering love; and the
servant, who represents both fallen humanity and the crucified Christ, 'beholds' us in our sin. Later Julian 'beholds' the
lord and servant again:

Another marvel was that this great lord had no servant but
one, and him he sent away. I beheld, thinking what manner
of labour it might be that the servant should do. And then
I understood that he should do the greatest labour and
hardest travail that there is – he should be a gardener;
delving and dyking, toiling and sweating, and turning the
earth upside-down, and seeking the depths, and watering
the plants in due time. (LT 51)

It is in this context that Julian comes to call Jesus, and even
God, our mother: Christ is our mother because we have our
being through him (or her), because he feeds and sustains us,
but above all because he suffers for and with us, transforming
our frailty and sinfulness from within. Julian unhesitatingly
applies this idea to the Trinity too:

I saw and understood that the high might of the Trinity is
our father, and the deep wisdom of the Trinity is our
mother, and the great love of the Trinity is our lord . . .

96

And furthermore I saw that the second person, who is our mother in respect of our substance, that same beloved person has become our mother in respect of our sensuality; for we are created by God to be of a double nature – that is to say, substantial and sensual. Our substance is the higher part, which we have in our father, God almighty; and the second person of the Trinity is our mother by nature, in virtue of having created our substance, and in whom we are grounded and rooted. And he is [also] our mother by mercy, in virtue of having taken our sensuality [upon himself]. [LT 58]

Julian is concerned to express the unconditional nature of God's identification with us in the suffering Christ, drawing us back towards him, not by compulsion but by love. Just as God's nature is shot through with paradox – God is both courteous and homely, worthy both of our 'dread' and of our love – so too is ours: we have both 'substance' and 'sensuality'; the former is broadly our spiritual nature – our whole lives seen and lived in the perspective of God's love for us; and the latter is our 'worldly' nature – our whole lives seen and lived in the perspective of this world alone. (The distinction has much in common with St Paul's distinction of spirit and flesh.) And God is in both of them, intimately identified in Jesus with every aspect of human life, even to the extent of arranging our excretion system (LT 6).

Yet all this only emphasizes the force of the question referred to earlier: if God really loves us and wants us to be happy, then why permit sin and evil and all that disfigures the created world? It is essential to an understanding of Julian's spirituality to realize not only that she asks this question, but that her 'beholding' of God – indeed her entire work – is in a crucial sense the answer to it:

After this the lord brought to my mind the longing that I had for him earlier, and I saw that nothing hindered me but sin, and so I beheld generally in all of us. And I thought that if sin had not existed, we should all have been clean and like to our lord, as he made us; and thus, in my folly, before this time I often wondered why the origin of sin was not prevented by God's great foreseeing wisdom; for then, I thought, all should have been well . . . But Jesus, who informed me in this vision of all that I needed, answered thus: 'Sin is expedient, but all shall be well, and all shall be well, and all manner of thing shall be well.' In this bare word 'sin' our lord brought to my mind generally all that is not good, and the shameful despite and the utter noughting [being set at naught] that he endured for us in this life, and his dying, and all the pains and passions of all his creatures, spiritual and physical. (LT 27)

The reference here to her own folly can deceive: this is the prayer of protest in its sharpest and most piercing form, the subtle probes of Julian's questions reaching to the heart of the Christian mystery. Sin, notice, stands for 'all that is not good', not simply for deliberate evil; but Jesus' answer, that it is expedient or necessary, in other words that it is an inevitable consequence of our nature and freedom as human beings, apparently fails to satisfy. Julian 'beholds' further, and protests again:

But in this I stood beholding generally, sorrowfully and mourning, saying thus to our lord in my meaning with very great dread: 'Ah! Good lord, how can all be well in view of the great hurt that is come through sin to creatures?' And here I desired, as far as I dared, to have some more open declaration by which I might be at ease in this. (LT 29)

Christ answers her 'very meekly, and with very lovely comfort': the relationship between them is characterized not by passive self-denying 'contemplation' but by a dialectic of penetrating directness. Julian comes to see that we can never understand the whole mystery of evil in this life (LT 30); but this does not stop God from assuring her again that he will make all things well (LT 31), nor Julian from speculating about the future of those who are damned (LT 32) and later about that of a particular person whom she had loved (LT

35). In the end she comes to see that, in identifying with the extremities of human suffering, God transforms it so that our 'wounds' become 'worships' (or marks of honour) (LT 39); and the more we suffer the more we will be rewarded. In no sense does this imply that sin or evil are good things; but it does imply that, in the light of the crucified Christ, they are shared things; God suffers in every tortured creature, not only by feeling compassion (as the lord does for the servant) but by physically undergoing the ultimate experience of pain. God does not just send the servant: he *is* the servant; and in the agonized mother-creator who also becomes our slave the innermost heart of the divine love stands at last revealed.

What are the implications of Julian's 'beholding' for us? It will by now be clear that the word carries its own protest against all attempts to domesticate or restrict the focus of Christian contemplative prayer. It is illuminating to compare its use in Julian's work with the story in the gospels of Jesus encountering a rich young man who asks him what he must do to inherit eternal life. Jesus 'looked steadily at him and loved him' (Mark 10:21 JB) – though that did not prevent him from giving the man some sternly uncompromising advice. Throughout the gospels, Jesus 'sees' or beholds people whole, not superficially or two-dimensionally. St John describes Jesus as he went along 'seeing' a man who had been born blind (John 9:1). The disciples see him as well; but where they see only an object to theorize about, Jesus sees a human being in desperate need. The disciples' 'beholding' leads them to explain the situation (John 9:2): Jesus' 'beholding' leads him to *change* it. In a harassed and frenetic society we have largely lost this capacity of looking steadily or directly at people or situations, probing to the heart of the matter and seeking out the inner reality behnd the outer covering, the 'substance' as well as the 'sensuality'. Yet this is precisely what Julian means by 'beholding'. There is a strange and tragic irony in a society whose technology equips people to see the full horror, say, of an African famine, but whose capacity to behold, to look steadily at and engage with such a sight is appallingly stunted and impoverished. If we have little sense of God it may be that we are looking for him in the wrong places, and that when he is presented to our eyes in the heart of the world's suffering we have neither the strength nor the willingness to behold him. And those who are able, like Julian, to 'look steadily' and unflinchingly at the very people or situations that articulate the most difficult questions and demand the most deeply-felt protest, may find themselves staring at the contours of the crucified God.

In the writings of Julian of Norwich 'contemplation' – indeed all Christian prayer – is shown, as it were, in its true and indelible colours – not as a pious escape from the world's ills but as a painful and even protesting reflection on their nature, in the light of the love which alone can give them meaning. Julian was not a 'radical' or even a contemplative in the sense in which those words are sometimes used: she was, emphatically, a deeply orthodox Christian, not avoiding or smoothing away the raw wounds of human suffering but struggling to 'behold' them in the context of a loving and suffering God. And the persistent and childlike beholding of both evil and God, refusing to separate them or to take refuge in one from the other, or to evade the difficult questions they raise, bequeathed to the world an extraordinary new understanding of both. Julian's conclusion, with its characteristic blend of gentleness and resolute seeking after wisdom, is her enduring testimony:

> And beware that you do not take one thing after your affection and liking and leave another, for that is the condition of a heretic. But take everything together, and truly understand that all is according to holy scripture and grounded in the same, and that Jesus, our true love, light and truth, shall show to all pure souls who with meekness ask perseveringly for this wisdom from him. And you, to whom this book shall come, thank our saviour Christ halely and heartily that he made these showings and revelations for you, and to you, of his endless love, mercy and goodness, for your and our safe guide and conduct to everlasting bliss; which may Jesus most [surely] grant us. Amen. (LT 86)

FURTHER READING

The 'Revelations' exist in two versions: the earlier Short Text (ST), and the much fuller Long Text (LT), which Julian wrote perhaps twenty years later, and which contain much more extended reflections on her original visions. Julian wrote in Middle English; but with a little effort this is not difficult to follow, and richly rewards those who try: much is lost in most modern English translations. The most accessible text is: Marion Glasscoe (ed.), *Julian of Norwich: A Revelation of Love*, LT only (Exeter, 1976). There is a modern translation of both short and long texts, with full introduction, by Edmund Colledge and James Walsh, *Julian of Norwich, 'Showings'*, (Classics of Western Spirituality, London, SPCK, 1978).

Julia Gatta, *A Pastoral Art: spiritual guidance in the English mystics*. London, DLT, 1987.

Grace Jantzen, *Julian of Norwich*. London, SPCK, 1987.

Benedicta Ward SLG, *Julian the Solitary*. Fairacres Publications, 1988.

Robert Llewelyn (ed.), *Julian: woman of our day*. London, DLT, 1985.

Simon Tugwell, *Ways of Imperfection* (London, DLT, 1984), ch. 16.

Brant Pelphrey, *Christ Our Mother*. London, DLT, 1989. A valuable discussion of Julian's concept of 'beholding' together with a comprehensive analysis of her thought.

7

The Interior Protest
St Teresa of Avila

Few of the greatest spiritual writers can touch the heart on first encounter: the limitations of translation, the differences of cultural milieu, and the influence or 'persona' with which each is associated, all obstruct or cloud our view. But St Teresa still can, for all the vastness of the chasm separating us from sixteenth-century Spanish convents: the vivid freshness of her imagery, the sharp pastoral sense that stamps even her most introspective chapters, and the sheer human attractiveness of her character set her apart from many massively learned writers, and entirely compensate for anything she lacks in systematic coherence.

Both the immediate and the wider context in which she wrote are essential to any understanding of her spirituality; and her own writings offer us more hints than those of Julian do in establishing what these were. It is clear, first, that she writes in no sanitized ivory tower immune from everyday concerns: in the earlier version of her 'Way of Perfection', written in *c.* 1566, her responsibilities as prioress of the Carmelite nuns of the Primitive Observance at Avila are only too evident: 'I really need leisure, and, as you see, I have so little opportunity for writing that a week passes without my putting down a word, and so I forget what I have said and what I am going to say next.'[1] Later in the same work she writes:

It is a long time since I wrote the last chapter and I have had no chance of returning to my writing, so that, without reading through what I have written, I cannot remember what I said. However, I must not spend too much time at this, so it will be best if I go right on without troubling

about the connection. For those with orderly minds . . .
many books have been written, and these are so good and
are the work of such competent people that you would be
making a mistake if you paid heed to anything about prayer
that you learned from me.[2]

Later still, and inimitably, she writes: 'I only wish I could
write with both hands, so as not to forget one thing while I
am saying another.'[3]

Her major works, then, were not conceived as academic
treatises, but as pastoral and spiritual guidance for her sisters;
and they arise directly from her own experience, and in
response to their own concerns. But the wider context is even
more important. The Spain of the mid-sixteenth century was,
as the great historian Fernand Braudel points out, 'socially,
economically and politically . . . plunged into chaos, racked
by deep discontents aggravated even further by a religious
crisis which was taken very seriously.'[4] Outbreaks of hetero-
doxy in various parts of the country led to some of the most
ferocious persecution of which even the Inquisition at the
height of its powers was capable.[5] Throughout St Teresa's
writings the influence of this almost totalitarian Catholicism
is evident: the writings themselves had to satisfy the eyes of
censors as severe as in many police states; and, last but
emphatically not least, it takes no crusading feminist to realize
that Teresa was living and writing in what must have been
one of the most uncompromisingly male-dominated societies
in our patriarchal civilization.

To explore something of St Teresa's spirituality without
reference to these daunting features of her time would be
about as profitable as to describe the topography of an Alpine
valley without mentioning the mountains. Occasionally hints
of their looming presence obtrude into the text: St Teresa
tells her sisters that if they are to make progress in their lives
they will have to 'strive like strong men until you die in the
attempt'[6] – in a male world they had little option if they
were to be taken seriously. More significant still is her telling
reference to contemporary marriage: 'When a woman has
made an unhappy marriage she does not talk about it or

103

complain of it, lest it should come to her husband's knowl-
edge; she has to endure a great deal of misery and yet has no
one to whom she may relieve her mind.'[7] It is important to
stress that St Teresa is not protesting about this situation
with a view to effecting changes in society: on the contrary,
she is here exhorting her nuns to suffer their mortifications
with the same patience as their married counterparts are
expected to do. Her protest is on an altogether deeper level:
she is seeking to offer her sisters a 'way of perfection' in a
hostile world, a source of fulfilment and meaning in a *spiritual*
marriage that few contemporary women could conceivably
expect to find in a physical one. The most crucial passage of
all in this regard comes at the end of her most famous work,
and explains its purpose:

> Although when I began to write what I have set down here
> it was with great reluctance ... I am very glad I did so
> now that it is finished, and I think my labour has been
> well spent ... And considering how strictly you are clois-
> tered, my sisters, how few opportunities you have of rec-
> reation and how insufficient in number are your houses, I
> think it will be a great consolation for you, in some of your
> convents, to take your delight in this Interior Castle, for
> you can enter it and walk about in it at any time without
> asking leave from your superiors.[8]

The spirituality of St Teresa, then, offered her sisters a way
of living which to us might appear negative and ascetic, but
which to them opened up otherwise undreamed-of possibilities: the love and freedom they could never discover in
exterior relationships could be sought from a God who dwelt
deep within themselves, in realms where even the most intrus-
ive of confessors could not gain access. This is not to imply that
her convents were crammed with muscular matriarchs defiantly
subverting chauvinist hierarchies. But it is to insist that the
genuine orthodoxy and subtle respectfulness that characterize
Teresa's writings may sometimes conceal from us a spirituality of protest as profound and persuasive as any more
overtly strident writer could offer. It might be appropriate to

begin with her approach to herself, as writer and as woman, and to those who alternately advised and criticized her.

Teresa's attitude to herself, and to those who criticize or correct her, reflects her pervasive humility. It is salutary to remember that for her, as for many writers before her, humility is more a theological virtue than a narrowly moral one: it implies an accurate and unflinching self-knowledge, an awareness both of one's personal sinfulness and of the divine potential that exists within us all.[9] Early in her autobiography she reflects, characteristically, on her own failings: 'It grieves me whenever I remember what good inclinations the Lord had given me, and how little I profited by them.'[10] Yet this does not prevent her later from valuing her experience of God sufficiently to wish that kings had experienced it too.[11] She records a significant moment when a number of learned men criticized her: 'They would ask me certain questions, which I answered plainly, though carelessly; and they then thought I was trying to instruct them and considered myself a person of learning.'[12] Teresa shares her anxieties with God, who comforts her and tells her what to say to her critics: indeed it is clear that these experiences of hostility only serve to strengthen her love for God and sense of intimacy with him.[13]

The portrait of Teresa that emerges from her autobiography is of a genuinely humble and instinctively generous person, only rarely driven to criticize her religious advisers or superiors, but with an interior conviction and strength that will not allow her to compromise where spiritual truths or insights are at stake. She asks God to deliver us from people mindful of their own honour;[14] and on one spectacular occasion addresses an aristocrat incorrectly.[15] And she tells her sisters that we must have 'a holy boldness, for God helps the strong, being no respecter of persons'.[16] In one splendid passage she complains about the fact that one seems to need a university professorship if one is to avoid displeasing important people in the world.[17] But elsewhere she warns her nuns not to be too easily shocked by those outside the religious life:

Let us look at our own shortcomings and leave other

people's alone; for those who live carefully ordered lives are apt to be shocked at everything and we might well learn very important lessons from the persons who shock us. Our outward comportment and behaviour may be better than theirs; but this, though good, is not the most important thing: there is no reason why we should expect everyone else to travel by our own road, and we should not attempt to point them to the spiritual path when perhaps we do not know what it is.[18]

This combination of interior strength and pastoral sensitivity is reflected in her attitude to herself as a woman. In her autobiography she expresses her puzzlement over the strength of the opposition to her new foundation: 'I was astonished at all the trouble that the devil was taking to hurt a few poor women'.[19] Later she tells us that the Lord gives visions and raptures more frequently to women than to men (which is why, she adds, they need good confessors: her writings are peppered with warnings against bad or inadequate ones).[20] At the outset of the 'Interior Castle' she writes tellingly:

> I was told by the person who commanded me to write that, as the nuns of these convents of Our Lady of Carmel need someone to solve their difficulties concerning prayer, and as ... women best understand each other's language ... anything I might say would be particularly useful to them.[21]

And in the earlier text of the 'Way of Perfection' she tells God that he did not despise women – indeed that he found 'more faith and no less love in them than in men', instancing the Virgin Mary as an exemplar.[22] There is a powerful passage in the 'Interior Castle' where (following traditional biblical exegesis) she describes Mary the sister of Martha enduring bitter criticism on her way to anointing Jesus at the house of Simon the Pharisee. It may be that she has in mind here the experience of her own sisters:

> And do you think it would be a trifling mortification to a woman in her position to go through those streets – perhaps

alone, for her fervour was such that she cared nothing how she went – to enter a house that she had never entered before and then to have to put up with uncharitable talk from the Pharisee and from very many other people, all of which she was forced to endure? . . . I assure you, sisters, that that better part [which Jesus said she had chosen] came to her only after sore trials and great mortification . . . The later years of her life, too, during which she was absent from Him, would have been years of terrible torment; so she was not always enjoying the delights of contemplation at the Lord's feet.[23]

In one of her lesser works she observes that Jesus raised Lazarus from the dead, not because he had asked for it but because a sinful woman had.[24] Perhaps the most penetrating summary of her self-perception as a woman, however, appears in the twenty-eighth chapter of the 'Way of Perfection': she reminds her sisters that 'we women are not learned', which is why they need help in realizing that 'we actually have something within us incomparably more precious than anything we see outside'. If God himself dwelt inside a woman, he could and did dwell inside them.[25]

This brings us to Teresa's own picture of God; and here too there is a tension between the awe-inspiring figure frequently described as 'Your Majesty', and the intimate spouse seeking to rapture us in the spiritual marriage. The tension is well expressed in a passage from her autobiography: 'Although He [Christ] is my Lord, I can talk to Him as to a friend, because He is not, I believe, like those whom we call lords on earth, and all of whose power rests upon an authority conferred on them by others.[26] She goes on to reflect that such lords are only intermittently accessible, and then rarely to the poor; but you can talk to God about anything; and he doesn't mind even when you complain to him, whereas an earthly king certainly would.[27] Certainly Teresa does not hesitate to protest when she feels like it, frequently with infectious vigour, as when she complains about the way he afflicts his lovers, and about his irritating habit of expecting her to do things she could not possibly manage: indeed at one point she scolds

God vigorously: 'He must either', she writes 'not tell me to do these things or help us in our need.'[28] God loves it when we are honest with him, treating him frankly and openly, and will reward us all the more when we are.[29] In a significant passage she explains the apparent tension: true humility has nothing to do with limp passivity:

> Avoid being bashful with God, as some people are, in the belief that they are being humble. It would not be humility on your part if the King were to do you a favour and you refused to accept it; but you would be showing humility by taking it, and being pleased with it, yet realizing how far you are from deserving it. A fine humility it would be if I had the Emperor of Heaven and earth in my house, coming to it to do me a favour and to delight in my company, and I were so humble that I would not answer His questions, nor remain with Him, nor accept what He gave me, but left Him alone. Or if He were to speak to me and beg me to ask for what I wanted, and I were so humble that I preferred to remain poor and even let Him go away, so that He would see I had not sufficient resolution.[30]

Like Julian then, or the psalmist, St Teresa's relationship with God is characterized both by genuine reverence and by protest; and, like them, the dialectic of protest has to do not only with complaining but also with bearing witness, laying bare before God your deepest worries or questions without fear or fawning. In short it is the relationship of bride and bridegroom: like her contemporary St John of the Cross, and St Bernard (among many others) before them, St Teresa makes much use of the themes and images of the Song of Songs; and fired with the concept of God as divine spouse she can describe the summit and goal of human life as a spiritual marriage.

It is important to note that the journey of the soul towards this ultimate union is in no sense intended to be an élitist pilgrimage for the favoured few. St Teresa tells us that 'there are really very few' who do not reach at least the Fifth Mansion out of the seven which comprise her Interior Castle, even though it may be that she means few of those who originally set out, rather than of humankind generally.[31] More important still is what she says at the end of the 'Interior Castle', where she calls on her sisters to pray for those who have sinned and been forgiven: 'We must not think of souls like theirs as mean and insignificant; for each is an interior world, wherein are the many and beauteous Mansions that you have seen; it is reasonable that this should be so, since within each soul there is a mansion for God.'[32] 'Within *each* soul', not just within her soul or those of her sisters: indeed she frequently scolds them for thinking they are better than others outside the convent. This is not, of course, to say that the journey within will be easy: it will require a clear self-knowledge and humility, as we have seen – St Teresa tells us that most of our restlessness derives from not understanding ourselves;[33] and in the Sixth Mansion she stresses the vital importance of self-knowledge and humility when the soul is 'raptured' by the Spouse.[34] And only those who are able to seek an unambiguous and ascetic detachment from the things of the world are likely to be fit for the rigorous demands of the interior journey. Yet this detachment in no way excludes active love and service of neighbour: indeed St Teresa tells her sisters that the best way of dealing with interior trials is by becoming involved in active works of charity.[35] The searchingly introspective dimensions of her spirituality are balanced by her repeated emphasis on pastoral concern and love of others; and she once puckishly reproached her great Carmelite contemporary St John of the Cross for not remembering this:

This Father . . . gives some remarkably sound doctrine for those who are thinking of following the Exercises practised in the Company of Jesus, but it is not to our purpose. It would be a bad business for us if we could not seek God until we were dead to the world. Neither the Magdalen, nor the woman of Samaria, nor the Canaanitish woman was dead to the world when she found Him . . . God deliver me from people who are so spiritual that they want to turn everything into perfect contemplation, come what may.[36]

It is striking that Teresa adduces in support of her criticism three biblical women, and striking too that she rejects any idea that 'contemplation' implies an absolute separation from this world, however much she agrees with St John of the Cross that it is a sinful and transient place. There is a passionate protest in the 'Interior Castle' against such a search for private perfection:

> When I see people very diligently trying to discover what kind of prayer they are experiencing and so completely wrapt up in their prayers that they seem afraid to stir, or to indulge in a moment's thought, lest they should lose the slightest degree of the tenderness and devotion which they have been feeling, I realize how little they understand of the road to the attainment of union. They think that the whole thing consists in this. But no, sisters, no; what the Lord desires is works. If you see a sick woman to whom you can give some help, never be affected by the fear that your devotion will suffer, but take pity on her: if she is in pain, you should feel pain too; if necessary, fast so that she may have your food, not so much for her sake as because you know it to be your Lord's will. That is true union with His will.[37]

It is particularly striking that, in the seventh and innermost mansion of the Interior Castle, St Teresa produces her most eloquent protest against the kind of pseudo-holiness that involves a tacit rejection of others:

> Do you know when people really become spiritual? It is when they become the slaves of God and are branded with His sign, which is the sign of the Cross, in token that they have given Him their freedom. Then He can sell them as slaves to the whole world, as He himself was sold, and if He does this He will be doing them no wrong but showing them no slight favour. Unless they resolve to do this, they need not expect to make great progress. For the foundation of this whole edifice, as I have said, is humility, and, if you have not true humility, the Lord will not wish it to reach

any great height: in fact, it is for your own good that it should not; if it did, it would fall to the ground. Therefore, sisters, if you wish to lay good foundations, each of you must try to be the least of all, and the slave of God, and must seek a way and means to please and serve all your companions. If you do that, it will be of more value to you than to them and your foundation will be so firmly laid that your Castle will not fall.[38]

So the God of St Teresa is both king and friend, both creator and spouse: although she nowhere refers to God as mother, she does not hesitate to use some strikingly maternal images of him, such as the passage in the Interior Castle where she says that 'from those Divine breasts, where it seems that God is ever sustaining the soul, flow streams of milk, which solace all who dwell in the Castle.'[39] In her description of the Prayer of Quiet Teresa describes the soul as being 'like an infant at its mother's breast: such is the mother's care for it that she gives it its milk without its having to ask for it so much as by moving its lips'.[40] In approaching such a God what is needed, then, is not only humility but a childlike trust that is precisely the mark of the genuinely mature and 'strong' person Teresa wants her sisters to become: no one is such a giant, she says, that he or she does not need to become a child at the breast again.[41] But that is not all that is needed: the interior journey is too fraught with hazards and pitfalls to be undertaken without the services of an experienced guide. We have already seen that Teresa was quite ready to criticize confessors and others where necessary. But she none the less attached great importance to spiritual direction; and it is entirely characteristic that she should advise her sisters to treat their confessors with the same frankness as they were to use with God who, she says, is 'very anxious for us to speak candidly and clearly to those who are in His place, and to desire them to be acquainted wth all our thoughts, and still more with our actions, however trivial these may be'.[42]

At the heart of the interior journey, however, lies St Teresa's emphasis on the humanity of Christ; and it is by means of our own 'beholding' of this (to use Julian's word) that we draw closer to the spiritual marriage for which we were made. Teresa protests against those who reject Christ's humanity as too earthly and inappropriate for the contemplative life, and in a long and important chapter in her autobiography she explains why this matters: we are not angels, she says, and we have bodies, so there is nothing to be gained by pretending we haven't. Her marvellous insistence, in the same chapter, on the fact that God wants us to become like little donkeys drawing a water-wheel, must have raised a few ecclesiastical eyebrows among her early readers.[43] The same emphasis recurs throughout her work: in the Sixth Mansion of the Interior Castle she writes: 'However spiritual you are, you must not flee so completely from corporeal things as to think that meditation on the most sacred Humanity can actually harm you.'[44]

The goal of such meditation is the spiritual marriage, the inseparable union of God with the human soul the fullness of which can be experienced only after death. Indeed in order to experience it at all we have to die: in the Fifth Mansion St Teresa uses the image of a silkworm dying in becoming a butterfly, and in the Seventh Mansion even the butterfly has to die in order to be transformed into something inconceivably greater. We are created for this transformation, even though we cannot achieve it on our own: we are all silkworms, then butterflies, restless with longing for our divine spouse and homeland. And when or if we achieve the spiritual marriage we will be characterized first by self-forgetfulness – not the abnegation of self so much as the unconditional willingness to do what God wants; secondly by a 'desire to suffer' as Christ did, to love our enemies and to serve Christ in whatever ways we can; and thirdly by a longing to leave this world and live with God in peace for ever.

This unequivocal desire for heaven may appear to diminish all that has been said about St Teresa's pastoral concern and her emphasis upon love of neighbour, by comparison with the more strictly self-absorbed contemplation which underlies the thought of St John of the Cross. It is certainly true that to portray Teresa as anything other than a thoroughgoing ascetic would be grossly to misrepresent all that she stood for; and in this respect at least the two great Carmelite saints have much in common. But it is essential here to return to where we started, for we are even more likely to misrepresent her if we forget the context in which she lived and wrote. For the small communities of women religious which she founded and tended with such energy and love, this radical detachment from the values and customs of this world was the only way to holiness and joy; but it is also the prayer of protest in perhaps its most dramatic form. The longing for heaven, the careful and costly renunciation of earthly temptations, was a far more subtle and penetrating challenge to contemporary Christianity than the sporadic heresies that came and went; and it presupposed, not a lack of concern for other people but exactly the opposite. At the end of the Interior Castle St Teresa once more reminds her readers that even the highest form of contemplative love is diabolical unless it issues in costly love for others: speaking of St Paul, she writes:

> We can see in his life the effects of genuine visions and of contemplation coming from Our Lord and not from human imagination or from the deceit of the devil. Do you imagine that he shut himself up with his visions so as to enjoy those Divine favours and pursue no other occupation?[45]

It seems appropriate to end with some passages from her two greatest works which may serve to gather together the themes that have been explored and to underline their enduring relevance and power. She begins the twenty-sixth chapter of the 'Way of Perfection' by telling her sisters that, if they are to make progress, they will need someone to keep them company – and who better than Christ himself:

> Imagine that this Lord Himself is at your side and see how lovingly and how humbly He is teaching you – and, believe me, you should stay with so good a Friend for as long as you can before you leave Him. If you become accustomed to having Him at your side, and if He sees that you love Him to be there and are always trying to please Him, you will never be able, as we put it, to send Him away, nor

will He ever fail you. He will help you in all your trials and you will have Him everywhere. Do you think it is a small thing to have such a Friend as that beside you?[46]

Teresa makes it clear that she is not expecting them to think about Jesus or to conceptualize him, or 'to make long and subtle meditations with your understanding'. Instead she says, 'I am asking you only to look at Him.' This is not a matter of religious techniques, still less of scholarly study, but of a capacity to *look at*, to behold, and in the process to discover that Christ is already looking at us: we are very close here to Julian of Norwich's stress on 'beholding' which was explored in Chapter 6. There follows a passage of immense power:

A wife, they say, must be like this if she is to have a happy married life with her husband. If he is sad, she must show signs of sadness; if he is merry, even though she may not in fact be so, she must appear merry too. See what slavery you have escaped from, sisters! Yet this, without any pretence, is really how we are treated by the Lord. He becomes subject to us and is pleased to let you be the mistress and to conform to your will . . . Is it such a great thing that you should turn your eyes but once and look upon Him Who has made you such great gifts?[47]

Teresa continues by telling her sisters to meditate on the risen Christ if they are full of joy, on the crucified Christ in times of trial, and above all to be like Mary Magdalene at the foot of the cross, looking death 'straight in the face'.[48] And she tells them also simply to get used to *talking* to Jesus, for without that constant two-way communication any relationship will wither away: 'if words do not fail you when you talk to people on earth, why should they do so when you talk to God?'[49]

Here then, is the essence of St Teresa's spirituality in its most characteristic and challenging form: characteristic because it illustrates to perfection her vivid style, her use of clear and evocative images, her pervasive pastoral sensitivity and above all her own lived experience of a God who was also a friend; yet also challenging, because she summoned her sisters to something far more wonderful than anything they might expect to encounter in contemporary Spain: a God who had become not only a spouse but also a slave, who longed for his creatures to look at him with the same costly and unconditional love as that with which he looked and looks at them, and whose grace empowered those who responded to look even death in the face without fear. Few, if any, writers have lived and shared the heart of Christianity's good news without compromise or apology, and with such transforming joy as the little prioress from Avila, calling her silkworms to become butterflies:

> Here, then, daughters, you see what we can do, with God's favour. May His Majesty Himself be our Mansion as He is in this Prayer of Union which, as it were, we ourselves spin. When I say he will be our Mansion, and we can construct it for ourselves and hide ourselves in it, I seem to be suggesting that we can subtract from God, or add to Him. But of course we cannot possibly do that! We can neither subtract from, nor add to, God, but we can subtract from, and add to, ourselves, just as these little silkworms do. And, before we have finished doing all that we can in that respect, God will take this tiny achievement of ours, which is nothing at all, unite it with His greatness and give it such worth that its reward will be the Lord Himself. And as it is He Whom it has cost the most, so His Majesty will unite our small trials with the great trials which He suffered, and make both of them into one.[50]

NOTES

1 'Way of Perfection' 15 (vol. II, p. 59). All references are to *The Complete Works of Saint Teresa of Jesus*, tr. E. Allison Peers, 3 vols. London, Sheed & Ward, 1946, repr. 1982.
2 ibid. 19 (vol. II, p. 76).
3 ibid. 20 (vol. II, p. 88). This is also taken from the earlier text

of this work, written for the Avila nuns; the later text, intended for wider circulation, omits some of these homely asides.

4   *The Mediterranean and the Mediterranean World in the Age of Philip II*, vol. II (London, Collins, 1972), p. 954.

5   ibid. pp. 955ff.

6   'Way of Perfection' 20 (vol. II, p. 86). The same point is made in ch. 7 (vol. II, p. 35).

7   'Way of Perfection' 11 (vol. II, p. 47).

8   'Interior Castle' VII.4 (vol. II, p. 350).

9   cf., e.g., ibid. IV.1, 'Most of these trials and times of unrest come from the fact that we do not understand ourselves' (vol. II, p. 234); and VII.1, 'within each soul there is a mansion for God' (vol. II, p. 331).

10   'Life', Prologue (vol. I, p. 11).

11   ibid. 21 (vol. I, p. 131).

12   ibid. 28 (vol. I, p. 187).

13   ibid. 29 (vol. I, pp. 188–90); cf. also ibid. 25 (vol. I, pp. 162–4).

14   'Way of Perfection' 12 (vol. II, p. 52); cf. also 'Life' 21 (vol. I, p. 134).

15   'Way of Perfection' 22 (vol. II, p. 92).

16   ibid. 16 (vol. II, p. 68). She makes the same point in her 'Book of the Foundations' 29 (vol. III, p. 177).

17   'Life' 37 (vol. I, p. 266).

18   'Interior Castle' III.2 (vol. II, p. 229).

19   'Life' 36 (vol. I, p. 256).

20   ibid. 40 (vol. I, p. 293). For comments on confessors see, e.g., ibid. 5 (vol. I, p. 27).

21   'Interior Castle', Introduction (vol. II, p. 200).

22   'Way of Perfection' 3 (vol. II, p. 13).

23   'Interior Castle' VII.4 (vol. II, p. 349).

24   'Exclamations of the Soul to God' 10 (vol. II, p. 411).

25   'Way of Perfection' 28 (vol. II, pp. 117–18).

26   'Life' 37 (vol. I, p. 263).

27   ibid. 37 (vol. I, pp. 264–6).

28   'Interior Castle' VI.11 (vol. II, p. 326); 'Book of the Foundations' 18 (vol. III, p. 88); and ibid. 19 (vol. III, p. 96).

29   'Way of Perfection' 37 (vol. II, p. 162).

30   ibid. 28 (vol. II, pp. 114–15).

31   'Interior Castle' V.1 (vol. II, p. 247).

32   ibid. VII.1 (vol. II, p. 331).

33   ibid. IV.5 (vol. II, p. 234).

34   ibid. VI.10 (vol. II, p. 296).

35 ibid. VI.1 (vol. II, p. 274).
36 'Judgment Given by Saint Teresa upon Various Writings on the Words: "Seek Thyself in Me" ' (vol. III, p. 267). See Peers's introductory comments in vol. III, pp. 215–16.
37 'Interior Castle' V.3 (vol. II, p. 263).
38 ibid. VII.4 (vol. II, p. 347).
39 ibid. VII.2 (vol. II, p. 336).
40 'Way of Perfection' 31 (vol. II, pp. 130–1). See also her 'Conceptions of the Love of God' 4 (vol. II, p. 384).
41 'Life' 13 (vol. I, p. 80).
42 'Interior Castle' VI.9 (vol. II, pp. 317–18).
43 'Life' 22 (vol. I, pp. 136–44).
44 'Interior Castle' VI.7 (vol. II, p. 308).
45 ibid. VII.4 (vol. II, p. 345).
46 'Way of Perfection' 26 (vol. II, p. 106).
47 ibid. 26 (vol. II, p. 107).
48 ibid. (vol. II, p. 109).
49 ibid.
50 'Interior Castle' V.2 (vol. II, p. 254).

FURTHER READING

The complete works of St Teresa are available in two translations, both with useful introductions and notes: tr. E. Allison Peers, 3 vols, London, Sheed & Ward, 1946, rep. 1982; and tr. Kieran Kavanaugh and Otilio Rodriguez, 3 vols, Classics of Western Spirituality, London, 1979.

E. W. Trueman Dicken, *The Crucible of Love*. London, DLT, 1963.
Ruth Burrows, *The Interior Castle Explored*. London, Sheed & Ward, Veritas Publications, 1982.

8

The Pilgrim's Protest
John Bunyan

Strange contradictions mark the condition of religion in modern society. Many who believe in a God rarely visit a church. Many more have recourse to the language of prayer, calling upon this God at times of crisis, without ever pausing to consider what kind of a God they are calling on – probably because for most of the time they never feel the need to do so. It would be pleasant, and comforting, to decide from within the Christian fold that this is simply their fault: one more tragic consequence of a self-absorbed and epicurean society happily heedless of either hubris or heaven. It would also be wrong. 'If God seems far away,' proclaimed one wayside pulpit, 'guess who's moved?' What the pulpit omits to tell you is that *it* has moved too.

One indication of this shift is in the use of language. Whatever the limitations of its theology the 1662 Anglican Book of Common Prayer did at least address the issues of its day, and in language that was laced with the vivid imagery of everyday life: with its graphic prayers for rain or harvest or victory or protection at sea, it offered a genuinely lay spirituality, articulating the needs and fears of people where they were – in the street, in the home, in the fields or at battle, not simply in the pew. There is more than a whiff of clericalism about many modern productions, whatever the improvements in clarity and variety they offer. There are more prayers for 'ministry' and 'sacred ministry' in the 1980 Alternative Service Book than there are for peace, love and freedom put together. And the language, though happily free of some of the gloomier excesses of 1662, rarely evokes the everyday: the Prayer Book's General Confession, telling God that we 'have erred and strayed from thy ways like lost sheep', used an image that the smallest child could grasp; but its modern replacement, declaring that we have sinned 'through negligence, through weakness, through our own deliberate fault', evokes the committee-room rather than the marketplace. This might not matter – indeed it would be simply a cheap jibe – if the church as a whole had found other ways of addressing and articulating people's deepest needs and experiences. It is not at all clear that it has. The reason so many fail to appear regularly in churches is not only because they do not like being challenged, but also because they do not like being bored. And the pulpit that used to thunder on the street corners now bleats in the nave. It is not only the people that have moved. The church has too. And because both have, on the whole, moved *inwards*, becoming more persistently self-absorbed (not, as with de Foucauld or St Teresa, in order to challenge the world but simply in order to escape it), it is not surprising if the relationship between them has crumbled.

Diagnosis of course is easier than cure; and taking refuge in the past is easier than either. But if there were ever a person who would be turning in his grave at the Church's current predicament, itching to get back into the pulpit and preach the gospel in language that managed both to address people where they were and to scale the heights of English prose style, it would be John Bunyan, the tinker from Bedford. While the Church of England's ecclesiastics were busy producing the 1662 Book of Common Prayer, Bunyan was in Bedford gaol literally dreaming up what proved to be no less a literary and spiritual masterpiece: *The Pilgrim's Progress*. His relevance for a study of prayer as protest might be questioned: his own understanding of prayer, as will be seen, is as much a cry for grace and mercy as a challenge to God, though it is very far from being the grovelling self-abasement for which Puritan spirituality is usually (and unfairly) criticized. Yet the spirit of protest imbues all his writing: protest against sin and injustice, against all religion that formalizes and even denies access to God, and against all within the self that cuts a person off from the free grace and salvation that alone brings hope and happiness, even if (in Bunyan's view) only

to the elect. To a greater extent than any writer we have yet
explored, Bunyan writes for the unjustly afflicted, not simply
because he felt sorry for them but because he was one of
them; and the dark perspectives of Calvinist orthodoxy within
which he wrote do little to diminish (and in some senses
underline) the force of what he has to say.

It should be said at once that there is much dispute about
how far the great seventeenth-century Puritan preachers like
Bunyan succeeded in having an effect on the lives and life-
styles of the poor, though it has recently been argued strongly
that they did.[1] What is not in dispute is the effort they devoted
to doing so, as well as to protesting against all who patronized
or oppressed them. Bunyan's works constantly testify to this:
Christiana, the heroine of the second part of *The Pilgrim's
Progress*, is a 'poor woman' who sets out on her difficult
journey despite being taunted by her neighbour as being
'unwomanly';[2] and the brother-in-law of her companion
Mercy, a 'professor' or learned person (or perhaps simply
someone who 'professed' to be a Christian), publicly divorces
and ejects his wife because she persisted in showing kindness
to the poor.[3] In Bunyan's later allegory, *The Life and Death of
Mr Badman* (1680), he attacks those who take advantage of
the poor by extortion or any other means: it is 'a grinding of
their faces, a buying and selling of them';[4] and his graphic
work *A Few Sighs from Hell* (1658) contains a fierce critique
of the rich and powerful who do this. More significant for our
purposes, however, is what Bunyan says in *Instruction for the
Ignorant* (1675):

Q.   Whose prayers be they that God will hear?
A.   The prayers of the poor and needy.[5]

By 'the poor' Bunyan clearly means both the poor in body
and the poor in spirit; and his protest is directed against all
who exploit or misdirect either. One of the most vivid
moments in *The Pilgrim's Progress* is the description of Christian's and Faithful's experiences at Vanity Fair, where Faithful is accused of condemning the practices of all the nobility
and gentlemen of the town, as a result of which he is horribly

executed. But Bunyan put his trust in a God who would vindicate the poor, not only in allegory nor even simply after death, but here and now.[6] There is a crucial passage earlier in *The Pilgrim's Progress* where Charity tells Christian about the crucified Christ:

> And besides, there were some of them of the household that said they had seen, and spoke with him since he did die on the Cross; and they have attested that they had it from his own lips, that he is such a lover of poor pilgrims that the like is not to be found from the east to the west. They moreover gave an instance of what they affirmed, and that was: he had stripped himself of his glory that he might do this for the poor; and that they heard him say and affirm that he would not dwell in the Mountain of Sion alone. They said moreover that he had made many pilgrims princes though by nature they were beggars born, and their original had been the dunghill.[7]

Bunyan's concern for the poor derives, then, from the theology that underlies it, as well as from his own experience. The latter requires some comment first. Apart from his fairly (though not exceptionally) humble origins, Bunyan lived through one of the stormiest periods in English history, taking a full part in the freedom afforded to dissenters by Cromwell's victory over Charles I to discuss and preach about religion and politics virtually without restriction – and suffering the consequences when, with the restoration of the monarchy (and with it the Church of England) in 1660, non-ordained lay preachers like Bunyan were arrested and imprisoned if they refused to desist.

It is not always easy for those of us accustomed to think of Anglicanism as virtually synonymous wth tolerance and comprehensiveness to recognize that this was not always so. In the space of a week during one summer I visited a 'mass rock' in southern Ireland where Roman Catholics were obliged illegally to celebrate mass at constant risk from Church of Ireland landowners, and a 'covenanters' rock' in southern Scotland where those who took their name from the

Presbyterian Solemn League and Covenant of 1643 were forced to worship, again at the risk of summary arrest and execution by the soldiers and gentry of the episcopalian Crown. Both are bleak and beautiful places on spectacular mountainsides offering commanding views of all possible approach routes: both are hard to find, and not at all promoted or popular. Yet their very obscurity heightens the sense of the holy: here, in Irish and Scottish wind and rain, groups of devout and poor Christians, Catholic and Presbyterian, risked their lives by their worship as surely as Jews did in Warsaw or adherents of the Baha'i faith did in Iran; and, whether it was offered in church Latin or Scottish dialect, this was the prayer of protest in its most stubborn and undiluted form.

Unlike his Scottish covenanting counterparts, Bunyan had no mountains to hide on, and doubtless would have refused to do so anyway. He also refused to stop preaching, and spent twelve years in prison; and, like St John of the Cross and so many other great writers, it was during his imprisonment that he wrote his two greatest works – *The Pilgrim's Progress* and his autobiographical reflections, *Grace Abounding to the Chief of Sinners*. Even after his release he was frequently under threat of arrest, was imprisoned again for a year in 1676, and yet had become a national hero both through his preaching and his writing. He died suddenly in 1688, ironically the year of the Glorious Revolution which was to usher in at least a measure of tolerance for dissenters.

His writings and his theology reflect the turmoil of his life. This is not the place to explore the nature of Bunyan's conversion experience as he reflects on it in *Grace Abounding*, though it is worth emphasizing how drawn-out it was: this was no sudden and irrevocable Damascus Road experience, but years of struggling with enormous yawning doubt and anxiety: am I saved and forgiven, or not? At times this causes him to cry out to God: 'Then breaking out in the bitterness of my soul, I said to myself, with a grievous sigh, How can God comfort such a wretch as I?'[8] No sooner does he appear to glimpse the peace of mind for which he yearns (and which in Calvinist theology is known as 'assurance') than he is again plunged into despair and uncertainty. At one point there is a wry reflection on some unhelpful spiritual guidance he receives:

> About this time I took an opportunity to break my mind to an ancient Christian; and told him all my case. I told him also that I was afraid that I had sinned the sin against the Holy Ghost; and he told me, he thought so too. Here therefore I had but cold comfort, but, talking a little more with him, I found him, though a good man, a stranger to much combat with the devil. Wherefore I went to God again as well as I could, for mercy still.[9]

Bunyan never lost this pervasive sense of personal fragility and unworthiness, and it marks all he wrote: the very first hazard Christian has to confront on his journey is the Slough of Despond, which grips him fast until someone else hauls him out. There is no road to salvation which does not begin with a painful recognition of your own fundamental sinfulness and inability to help yourself. And Bunyan is no glib crusader peddling the easy cliché that, once saved, your problems are behind you. There are two marvellous and moving passages in *Grace Abounding* with which many (perhaps, if they are honest, *all*) preachers will identify:

> Indeed I have been as one sent to them from the dead; I went myself in chains to preach to them in chains, and carried that fire in my own conscience that I persuaded them to beware of. I can truly say, and that without dissembling, that when I have been to preach, I have gone full of guilt and terror even to the pulpit door, and there it hath been taken off, and I have been at liberty in my mind until I have done my work, and then immediately, even before I could get down the pulpit stairs, have been as bad as I was before. Yet God carried me on, but surely with a strong hand: for neither guilt nor hell could take me off my work . . .

> Sometimes again, when I have been preaching, I have

been violently assaulted with thoughts of blasphemy, and strongly tempted to speak them with my mouth before the congregation. I have also at some times, even when I have begun to speak the Word with much clearness, evidence, and liberty of speech, yet been before the ending of that opportunity so blinded, and so estranged from the things I have been speaking, and have also been so straitened in my speech, as to utterance before the people, that I have been as if I had not known or remembered what I have been about; or as if my head had been in a bag all the time of the exercise.[10]

And yet it is precisely this thoroughgoing recognition of interior weakness that leads him to redemption, as he expresses with pithy acuteness in *Grace Abounding*: 'Great sins', he writes, 'do draw out great goodness'; and he realizes that 'God had a bigger mouth to speak with than had heart to conceive with.'[11] Merely protesting against sin is not enough, as Faithful points out in *The Pilgrim's Progress*;[12] but this honest self-perception is the indispensable starting-point for the Christian – and the greater the sinner, the greater God's loving concern.[13]

We can, then, do nothing to save ourselves other than acknowledge uncompromisingly our need of salvation: God can then, if he chooses, *impute* Christ's righteousness to us, as Bunyan explains in classic Calvinist language in *Grace Abounding*:

Now was I as one awakened out of some troublesome sleep and dream, and listening to this heavenly sentence, I was as if I had heard it thus expounded to me; Sinner, thou thinkest that because of thy sins and infirmities, I cannot save thy soul; but behold my Son is by me, and upon him I look, and not on thee, and will deal with thee according as I am pleased with him: at this I was greatly lightened in my mind, and made to understand that God could justify a sinner at any time, it was but looking upon Christ, and imputing of his benefits to us, and the work was forthwith done.[14]

The same point is made more vividly in *The Pilgrm's Progress*: Christian, who had been burdened with a heavy sense of sin from the start of his journey (symbolized by the pack he carries), loses his burden with dramatic suddenness as soon as he comes face to face with the crucified Christ.[15] He does nothing to deserve it: he simply has to accept it, having first accepted that he needs it; and it happens. It is not the end of his problems, any more (as we have seen) than conversion was the end of Bunyan's. But it transforms him all the same.

Now it is impossible to go further without recognizing that many will find this unrelenting Calvinism hard to swallow. The idea of a God who, with apparently arbitrary, almost whimsical exercise of freedom, predestines some and not others: the spectacle of someone who appears overridingly concerned with his own personal salvation; and the faint whiff of manipulation about a theory of redemption which provides detailed guidelines for the disposal of a heavy burden that most people had not hitherto felt any need to carry – all these aspects of Bunyan's thought may cause *us* to protest even more than he does. For our purposes, however, what matters is not so much the strengths and weaknesses of his theology as the spirituality to which both contribute.

For once this free gift of salvation is accepted God ceases to be simply a wrathful judge and becomes a friend. What we cannot possibly achieve on our own Christ achieves for us – free and direct access to, and intimacy with, God. In his later treatise *The Work of Jesus Christ as an Advocate* Bunyan stresses the enormous implications of this:

> As we should make use of Christ's advocateship for the strengthening of our faith, so we should also make use thereof to the encouraging us to prayer. As our faith is, so is our prayer; to wit, cold, weak, and doubtful, if our faith be so. When faith cannot apprehend that we have access to the Father by Christ, or that we have an Advocate, when charged before God for our sins by the devil, then we flag and faint in our prayer; but when we begin to take courage to believe – and then we do so when most clearly we apprehend Christ – then we get up in prayer. And

according as a man apprehends Christ in his undertakings and offices, so he will wrestle with and supplicate God.[16]

Once Christ is seen as our advocate – and as Bunyan points out earlier in the same work, as our friend[17] – we can begin to see prayer not simply as a cry for forgiveness but also (once that is heard) as an active and intimate engagement with God. It is these two ingredients which characterize Bunyan's understanding of prayer, and both are worth reflecting upon briefly.

We have already seen that Bunyan's perception of sin and evil led him not only to castigate the gross injustices of contemporary English society but also to probe his own guilt and wretchedness with painful accuracy – not every Christian writer has been as willing to acknowledge the beam in his own eye while readily pointing out those of others. In turn this leads to a spirituality that echoes the Psalms in being grounded in a cry for deliverance and mercy that was at once passionate and desperate. In his *Treatise of the Fear of God* (1679) Bunyan points out the positive dimension of a sense of personal unworthiness and fear of judgment: it leads to 'hearty, fervent and constant prayer'; and true fear 'will add boldness to his soul in his approaches into the presence of God.'[18] He explores this theme much more extensively in his most important text on prayer, the *Discourse on Prayer* (subtitled 'I will pray with the Spirit') of 1662, written from prison: right prayer 'bubbleth out of the heart when it is overpressed with grief and bitterness', as it did for Jesus; and Bunyan defines prayer itself as 'a pouring out of the heart or soul. There is in prayer an unbosoming of a man's self, an opening of the heart to God, an affectionate pouring out of the soul in requests, sighs, and groans.'[19]

Later in the same work he says that 'the best prayers have often more groans than words', and that the person praying out of bitterness and despair will be heard by God before the coolly posturing prelate reciting his set liturgical formulae.[20] This is a favourite theme of Bunyan's, as it was for many of his Puritan contemporaries: his constant protests against the learned, the clever and those who recite formal prayers, reflects both classic nonconformist principle and his own personal experience. In *The Pilgrim's Progress* Formalist and Hypocrisy (both, it should be noticed, members of the gentry, not poor people) are vigorously criticized by Christian for thinking that they were as acceptable to God as he even though they had not come in by the narrow gate; and in his powerful treatise *The Pharisee and the Publican* (1635) Bunyan proscribes 'they that use high and flaunting language in prayer'.[21]

Again however, it is in his *Discourse on Prayer* that he expresses his views most powerfully: 'A good sense of sin and the wrath of God, with some encouragement from God to come unto him, is a better common prayer-book than that which is taken out of the Papistical mass-book.'[22] Bunyan is perhaps unfair here to the 1662 Book of Common Prayer, which is not notably deficient in the qualities he advocates. Indeed for it, as for him, prayer is first a cry for help and mercy that is both the essential consequence of perceiving one's own sinfulness and implicitly a protest against those who have not perceived their own. In his last sermon, dated 19 August 1688 and preached in London, Bunyan makes this clear:

A child, you know, is incident to cry as soon as it comes into the world; for if there be no noise, they say it is dead. You that are born of God, and Christians, if you be not criers, there is no spiritual life in you – if you be born of God, you are crying ones; as soon as he has raised you out of the dark dungeon of sin, you cannot but cry to God, What must I do to be saved? . . . Oh! how many prayerless professors is there in London that never pray! Coffee-houses will not let you pray, trades will not let you pray, looking-glasses will not let you pray; but if you was born of God, you would.[23]

This, then, is the essential condition of Christian prayer – not the untroubled eloquence of the leisured and the literate but the urgent pleas of the anxious and the desperate. We are to complain to God, pouring out our troubles to him, as Bunyan also makes clear in his final sermon;[24] and in the *Discourse on Prayer* he answers the query of those who can never find the right words:

QUERY SECOND: Yea, but when I go into secret, and intend to pour out my soul before God, I can scarce say anything at all.

ANSWER: 1. Ah! sweet soul! it is not thy words that God so much regards, as that he will not mind thee, except thou comest before him with some eloquent oration. His eye is on the brokenness of thine heart; and that it is that makes the very bowels of the Lord to run over . . .

2. The stopping of thy words may arise from overmuch trouble in thy heart. David was so troubled sometimes, that he could not speak. But this may comfort all such sorrowful hearts as thou art, that though thou canst not through the anguish of thy spirit speak much, yet the Holy Spirit stirs up in thine heart groans and sighs, so much the more vehement: when the mouth is hindered, yet the spirit is not.[25]

It is not surprising that Bunyan, here as elsewhere, loves to quote the Psalms, for his spirituality is strikingly close to theirs. A Kuwaiti man, whose wife was among many hostages held for days during an airline hi-jack, expressed to newspaper reporters his sense of utter helplessness during those terrible hours of anxious waiting: the one thing he felt able to do for his wife was to pray; but he could not, for he had forgotten what words to use. He is not alone: in our own society, changes in religious education as well as lack of familiarity with the old texts of the Lord's Prayer or the King James Bible have deprived many of words that could be, and often were, sources of indispensable comfort *in extremis*. We do not need to accept Bunyan's critique of formal prayers to recognize, in this sense at least, the similarity of our situation and his – and to take seriously his answer. For prayer is not the preserve of the pious or the articulate; and if it consists of no more than the helpless scream of the bereaved or the bitter frustration of the destitute, it is enough.

And the reason it is enough is because of the nature of the God to whom it is addressed. Because we are accepted and justified, because Christ's death has opened the way to God, our cries for help are heard; and here Bunyan's spirituality is at its most powerfully paradoxical. The fearful, guilt-ridden, inarticulate sinner – of all people – can not only gain access to God: he can be bold and intimate and honest with him to a degree far beyond those smugly confident of their religious worth. Bunyan explores this theme frequently, but above all in his *Discourse on Prayer*: by virtue of our union with Christ, we can come to God boldly, standing upright in the strength of Christ's own intercessions on our behalf, confident of being heard not because *we* deserve to be but because Christ does. And this transforms our stuttering shrieks into incandescent eloquence. Bunyan makes the point in answer to a judge at his trial:

> ANOTHER JUSTICE: What do you count prayer? Do you think it is to say a few words over before, or among a people?

> BUNYAN: I said, no, not so; for men might have many elegant, or excellent words, and yet not pray at all: but when a man prayeth he doth through a sense of those things which he wants (which sense is begotten by the spirit) pour out his heart before God through Christ; though his words be not so many, and so excellent as others are.[26]

If God is our father and our friend, then we have no need of formal eloquence, any more than a child needs to declaim Shakespearean English in order to gain his or her parent's attention; as Geoffrey Nuttall has pointed out, people 'could come to God boldly and familiarly, as children to their Father', in the view of the Puritan divines.[27] Everyone has access to God, and the poor and needy most immediately of all.

Yet this is not to say that prayer will always be easy. On

the contrary: Bunyan, for all his emphasis on the priority of
the divine grace, frequently stresses that it will be very hard
work, requiring perseverance and stamina. There is a powerful reflection on this in his treatise *Christ a Complete Saviour*:

> Our prayers, how imperfect are they! With how much
> unbelief are they mixed! How apt is our tongue to run, in
> prayer, before our hearts! With how much earnestness do
> our lips move, while our hearts lie within as cold as cold!
> Yea, and ofttimes, it is to be feared, we ask for that with
> our mouth that we care not whether we have or no. Where
> is the man that pursues with all his might what but now
> he seemed to ask for with all his heart? Prayer is become
> a shell, a piece of formality, a very empty thing, as to the
> spirit and life of prayer at this day. I speak now of the
> prayers of the godly. I once met with a poor woman that,
> in the greatest of her distresses, told me she did use to rise
> in the night, in cold weather, and pray to God, while she
> sweat with fears of the loss of her prayer and desires that
> her soul might be saved. I have heard of many that have
> *played*, but of few that have *prayed*, till they have sweat, by
> reason of their wrestling with God for mercy.[28]

This is a vital point: however intense and passionate our
prayers, they need to be followed up by effort and striving to
achieve what it is that we have prayed for. In *The Pilgrim's
Progress* Christian and his companion pray all night in Giant
Despair's castle, and their prayer is answered by the sudden
discovery of a key; but they still have to make their way to
safety by their own efforts.[29] And sometimes our prayers will
have to be persevering, stubbornly persistent, in the face of
apparent silence from God:

> Here now, if the soul be not well informed in its understand-
> ing, it will presently cry out, 'the Lord hath forsaken me,
> and my Lord hath forgotten me'. Whereas the soul rightly
> informed and enlightened saith, Well, I will seek the Lord,
> and wait; I will not leave off, though the Lord keep silence,
> and speak not one word of comfort. He loved Jacob dearly,

and yet he made him wrestle before he had the blessing. Seeming delays in God are no tokens of his displeasure; he may hide his face from his dearest saints. He loves to keep his people praying, and to find them ever knocking at the gate of heaven.[30]

'He may hide his face from his dearest saints': Bunyan knew from painful personal experience how true that was; and millions before and after him, from the Roman circuses to the cattle trucks of Dachau, have known it too. In the end the tinker from Bedford had no clearer explanation than anyone else about why this should be, and was honest enough to say so. But it did not stop him hammering on the doors of heaven in the name of all those who have felt, as he did, the constant need for love and acceptance and companionship. The latter is as significant as the first two: it is a great mistake to think of Bunyan as a narrowly individualist writer, concerned only with his own private problems and personal salvation. On the contrary: it is precisely because he knows how greatly *he* needs help that he recognizes both his commitment to, and reliance upon, other people. There is a strongly corporate dimension to his spirituality, as he makes clear in the *Discourse on Prayer*;[31] and in *The Pilgrim's Progress* Christian tells Hopeful that one of the signs of the apostate is the way 'they shun the company of lively and warm Christians'.[32]

John Bunyan's prayer of protest, as we have seen, leaves many questions unanswered, foremost among them the strange nature of a God who appears to make the whole process of salvation so arbitrary and unfair. And yet it may be precisely this that makes his spirituality so relevant today; for we, like him, live in a world where life and society *are* arbitrary and unfair, where a few achieve meaning and wholeness while the many live and die without either, and where the Slough of Despond and Vanity Fair still claim far more lives than the journey to the Celestial City. And our response to that, like Bunyan's, must be to protest: against the corrosive structures of sin that exalt the complacent and the privileged (and, if we are honest, eat away at our own self-perception and integrity too) – and even at the God in whose name

131

so much of the world's evil is committed. It is no coincidence that Bunyan, who stressed so repeatedly the importance of the next world, never lost his prophetic commitment to the radical overhauling of this one, for in his vision the two belong inescapably together: when, in the tremendous climax of his great masterpiece, Mr Valiant-for-Truth passes over death and the trumpets sound for him on the other side, we are suddenly aware that his and his fellow-pilgrims' triumph is not simply a pious hope for the future, but a vivid blueprint for the present; and his famous hymn a protest and challenge to this world as well as a pledge of enduring confidence in the next:

> Hobgoblin, nor foul fiend,
> Can daunt his spirit:
> He knows he at the end
> Shall life inherit.
> Then fancies fly away,
> He'll fear not what men say,
> He'll labour night and day,
> To be a pilgrim.[33]

NOTES

1 See Eamon Duffy, 'The godly and the multitude in Stuart England', *Seventeenth Century*, vol. I, no. 1 (1986), pp. 31–55.
2 *The Pilgrim's Progress*, ed. Sharrock (London, Penguin, 1965, repr. 1987), pp. 239–40.
3 ibid. p. 291.
4 *The Life and Death of Mr Badman* (London, Everyman's Library, 1928, repr. 1956), p. 243.
5 *Instruction for the Ignorant*, ed. Offor, *The Works of John Bunyan* (Glasgow, Blackie, 1859), vol. II, p. 687.
6 'The Dissenters expected their sufferings to be rewarded not only by their own eternal happiness in the life to come, but also in the future prosperity of their cause here on earth', Michael Watts, *The Dissenters: from the Reformation to the French Revolution* (Oxford, Clarendon Press, 1978, repr. 1985), pp. 241–2.

7   *The Pilgrim's Progress*, p. 98.
8   *Grace Abounding*, ed. Owens (London, Penguin, 1965, repr. 1987), p. 49.
9   ibid. p. 46.
10 ibid. pp. 70, 73.
11 ibid. pp. 63–4.
12 *The Pilgrim's Progress*, p. 129.
13 See *The Jerusalem Sinner Saved* (1688), ed. Offor, vol. I, pp. 73ff.
14 *Grace Abounding*, pp. 65–6.
15 *The Pilgrim's Progress*, p. 81.
16 *The Work of Jesus Christ as an Advocate*, ed. Offor, vol. I, p. 196.
17 ibid. p. 172.
18 *A Treatise of the Fear of God*, ed. Greaves (Oxford University Press, 1981), pp. 70, 108.
19 *Discourse on Prayer*, ed. Offor, vol. I, pp. 624–5.
20 ibid. pp. 631, 633.
21 *The Pharisee and the Publican*, ed. Offor, vol. II, pp. 276–7.
22 *Discourse on Prayer*, p. 624.
23 *Mr Bunyan's Last Sermon*, ed. Offor, vol. II, p. 756.
24 ibid. p. 757.
25 *Discourse on Prayer*, pp. 634–5.
26 *A Relation of the Imprisonment of Mr John Bunyan*, ed. Owens (London, Penguin, 1987), p. 95.
27 *The Holy Spirit in Puritan Faith and Experience* (Oxford, Blackwell, 1946), p. 66.
28 *Christ a Complete Saviour*, ed. Offor, vol. I, p. 213.
29 *The Pilgrim's Progress*, p. 168.
30 *Discourse on Prayer*, p. 634.
31 ibid. pp. 626–7.
32 *The Pilgrim's Progress*, p. 206.
33 ibid. p. 367.

FURTHER READING

The complete works of John Bunyan are available in the edition of George Offor (Glasgow: Blackie & Son, 3 vols, 1859). The most accessible texts of *The Pilgrim's Progress* and *Grace Abounding to the Chief of Sinners* are the Penguin editions cited above.

Christopher Hill, *A Turbulent, Seditious and Factious People: John Bunyan and his Church*. Oxford University Press, 1988.

Christopher Hill, *The World Turned Upside Down*. London, Penguin, 1975.

Geoffrey F. Nuttall, *The Puritan Spirit*. London, Epworth, 1967.

Geoffrey F. Nuttall, *The Holy Spirit in Puritan Faith and Experience*. Oxford, Blackwell, 1946.

Michael Watts, *The Dissenters: from the Reformation to the French Revolution*. Oxford, Clarendon Press, 1978, repr. 1985.

Monica Furlong, *Puritan's Progress: a study of John Bunyan*. London, Hodder & Stoughton, 1975.

Vivienne Evans, *John Bunyan: his life and times*. Dunstable, Book Castle, 1988.

R. H. Tawney, *Religion and the Rise of Capitalism*. 1926.

The splendid essay by Lord Macaulay on John Bunyan is still well worth reading: Macaulay, *Critical and Historical Essays*, vol. II. London, Everyman's Library, 1907, repr. 1967.

9

The Land of Lost Content
The Poets of the First World War

The saddest thing I can recall was when the 1914 War was declared. Nearly all the young men went. They were the brothers of my school friends, with all of whom I had played Snakes and Ladders and Ludo on their kitchen table, before their mothers and fathers came home from work. We used to play by candlelight and when the candle was burnt down to the candle grease we had to watch it burn. We never seemed to get burnt – my mother used to say, 'God takes care of children'. These fair boys all joined the army to 'Save England' and nearly all were killed . . . So few came back. All were good brave young men, but I doubt if they knew what it was all about.[1]

These reminiscences of Alice Cordelia Davis from Camberwell in South London, born in 1898, vividly hint at some of the issues raised by the First World War: the unthinking and fervent patriotism, the disappearance of almost an entire generation of young men, and the grotesque disparity between a God that 'takes care of children' but seemed deaf to the cries of several million adults. Something more than crude jingoism died in the Passchendaele mud and the trenches by the Somme: the easy assumptions about the justness and glory of war, and about God's emphatic Englishness, died too, though they have been resurrected often enough since. The Housman poem that gives this chapter its title was written well before the war began; but its popularity after 1914 was not surprising: it was indeed a 'land of lost content' that came slowly to realize that no war, least of all this one,

135

could conceivably justify such almost unimaginable cost and suffering. In Susan Hill's moving novel *Strange Meeting*, the two young subalterns who have become friends at the Western Front discuss military tactics on the night before the tragic advance that forms the book's climax:

'By the next war, the message will have got through.'
'There will never be another war.'
'There will always be war.'
'Men couldn't be so stupid, John! After all this? Isn't the only real purpose of our being here to teach them that lesson – how bloody useless and pointless the whole thing is?'
'Men are naturally stupid and they do not learn from experience.'
'You haven't much faith in humanity.'
'Collectively, no.'
'Individually?'
'Oh, yes. You've only to look around you here.'[2]

Who was to blame, then, for allowing such a thing to happen: for letting Europe slide effortlessly into war, and for enabling the war machines of the Great Powers to grow into a huge hydra-headed monster that consumed the lives of millions for no discernible reason? What is it in human nature that permits so many individuals, most of whom would otherwise spend their lives enjoying their families and greeting strangers courteously in the street, to surrender their freedom and autonomy to a gigantic collective capable of indescribable horrors that most of them could never even have imagined, let alone have committed? It is of course fatally easy, from the comfortable perspective of sixty years on, to apportion blame and heap calumny in generous quantities upon all involved in the instigation and conduct of the Great War: it is also, in large measure, cruelly unfair. It is easy to deride the lumbering pomposities and sometimes inept judgments of generals like French or Joffre or Haig; and easy to forget how hopelessly unprepared and ill-equipped both they and their armies were for a gigantic and largely static four-year struggle in appalling conditions. It is even easier to criticize the windy rodomontade and xenophobic theology of someone like A. F. Winnington-Ingram, Bishop of London, who said in 1915:

> I think the Church can best help the nation first of all by making it realise that it is engaged in a Holy War, and not be afraid of saying so. Christ died on Good Friday for Freedom, Honour, and Chivalry, and our boys are dying for the same thing.[3]

Yet he was not the first, nor would be the last, church leader to deal with the difficult dilemma of distinguishing God's cause from the country's by simply declaring them to be one and the same. Even from our detached vantage-point, it is hard to see whom to blame for what happened in Europe between 1914 and 1918; and for those who were more perceptive than Winnington-Ingram, it was hard enough at the time. Perhaps, both then and now, there was only one person who could legitimately be held responsible, and to whom cries of protest and pleas for justice could appropriately be directed; and that was neither the luckless Kaiser Wilhelm II nor the teenage assassin of Franz Ferdinand at Sarajevo. It was God.

Attitudes to God during the First World War varied wildly. The problem of reconciling God with undeserved suffering was not, of course, new; and we have already explored the responses that the psalmists, Job and Julian of Norwich made to it. What was different was neither the problem nor the scale (both the sack of Jerusalem and the Black Death must have appeared equally cataclysmic in their times), but the world in which it happened. It was no longer so easy simply to blame it all on the 'enemy', as the psalmist had done, now that the royal houses of Great Britain and Germany were closely related and the Germans appeared to pray to the same God as the Church of England. Nor was it as simple as it had once been to declare that God was in control, that he must know what he was doing, and that no doubt everything would come together for the best. It is true that some still tried to hold on to a God like that, doubtless because no one

137

had ever suggested to them that such a God would be an ogre if he existed at all: one grieving mother wrote, after her son had been killed near Passchendaele in September 1917: 'When these Awful tidings are sent us it shakes our faith. But then again when we get calm we know that God is still in his heaven and He orders all things for the best.'[4] But others not unnaturally found that intolerable. Some, like the poet Edward Thomas, depicted God as sitting 'aloft in the array/ That we have wrought him, stone-deaf and stone-blind.'[5] Another poet, J. C. Squire, recognized God's uncomfortable predicament:

> God heard the embattled nations sing and shout:
> 'Gott strafe England' – 'God save the King' –
> 'God this – 'God that' – and 'God the other thing.'
> 'My God,' said God, 'I've got my work cut out.'[6]

The atheist writer H. H. Munro (Saki), himself a victim of the war, resorted to pithy satire:

> While shepherds watched their flocks by night
> All seated on the ground,
> A high-explosive shell came down
> And mutton rained around.[7]

And a little-known woman poet wrote a bitter denunciation of an omnipotent God in 1916:

> I shouted for blood as I ran, brother,
>   Till my bayonet pierced your breast;
> I lunged thro' the heart of a man, brother,
>   That the sons of men might rest.
>
> I swung up my rifle apace, brother.
>   Gasping with wrath awhile,
> And I smote at your writhing face, brother,
>   That the face of peace might smile.
>
> Your eyes are beginning to glaze, brother,
>   Your wounds are ceasing to bleed.

> God's ways are wonderful ways, brother,
> And hard for your wife to read.[8]

Our primary concern here, however, is not with the theological question but with the spiritual one: not with how people argued about the problem of God and suffering but with how they articulated that problem, and indeed all they saw and experienced, to whatever God they believed in. Although our exploration will be restricted to British writers, it is worth remembering that the problem (like the suffering) was not a monopoly of one side or country. In 'A White Low Sun' the Russian poet Marina Tsvetayeva challenges God with the stark ferocity of the psalmist:

> A white low sun, low thunderclouds; and back
> behind the kitchen-garden's white wall, graves.
> On the sand, serried ranks of straw-stuffed forms
> as large as men, hang from some cross-beam.
>
> Through the staked fence, moving about, I see
> a scattering: of soldiers, trees, and roads;
> and an old woman standing by her gate
> who chews on a black hunk of bread with salt.
>
> What have these grey huts done to anger you,
> my God? and why must so many be killed?
> A train passed, wailing, and the soldiers wailed
> as its retreating path got trailed with dust.
>
> Better to die, or not to have been born,
> than hear that plaining, piteous convict wail
> about these beautiful dark eyebrowed women.
> It's soldiers who sing these days. O Lord God.[9]

The English army chaplain Oswin Creighton underlines the point, imagining an officer saying to God: 'You have allowed the world to become an impossible place – a mass of contradictions'; and nine months before he was killed he wrote, 'I sometimes feel inclined to wonder why God hides Himself so inscrutably from our experience. Or is it that the Church has taught us for so long to look for Him in the wrong places?'[10]

Two questions, then, dominate the spirituality of the First World War and both are directed at God: why are you letting this happen? And where are you? Both appear prominently in the writings of three poets who require a more detailed examination, two of whom need no introduction: Siegfried Sassoon, Geoffrey Studdert Kennedy and Wilfred Owen.

References to God abound in the poetry of Siegfried Sassoon, though none is more powerful than a passage in his semi-autobiographical *Complete Memoirs of George Sherston*, where he mentions a pair of hands of unknown nationality, protruding from a trench: 'Every time I passed that place the protest of those fingers became more expressive of an appeal to God in defiance of those who made the War.'[11] Sassoon had little time for the efforts of army chaplains, or of clergy in general: elsewhere in the Memoirs he recalls a vicar saying to those going to France, 'And now God go with you. I will go with you as far as the station.'[12] Winnington-Ingram is crushingly dealt with in poems like 'Vicarious Christ', written in 1919, and even more in the visceral ferocity of his 1916 poem 'They':

> The Bishop tells us: 'When the boys come back
> They will not be the same; for they'll have fought
> In a just cause: they lead the attack
> On Anti-Christ; their comrades' blood has bought
> New right to breed an honourable race,
> They have challenged Death and dared him face to face.'
>
> 'We're none of us the same!' the boys reply.
> 'For George lost both his legs; and Bill's stone blind;
> Poor Jim's shot through the lungs and like to die;
> And Bert's gone syphilitic; you'll not find
> A chap who's served that hasn't found *some* change.'
> And the Bishop said: 'The ways of God are strange!'[13]

Yet it was not simply the failings of the church that preoccupied Sassoon. In early war poems like 'The Redeemer' he sees Christ in the heart of the soldiers' suffering, both identifying with them and in some sense consecrating their pain and making their struggles holy, albeit without any of the crude chauvinism of Rupert Brooke's poem 'Peace'.[14] It is an approach to the problem of war spirituality which was developed more fully by Studdert Kennedy. Sassoon, however, was not satisfied with it for long. In 'The Prince of Wounds', written only a month after 'The Redeemer', he again sees Christ in their midst; but this time his presence prompts more questions than it answers:

> The Prince of wounds is with us here;
> Wearing his crown he gazes down,
> Sad and forgiving and austere.
> We have renounced our lovely things,
> Music and colour and delight:
> The spirit of Destruction sings
> And tramples on the flaring night.
> But Christ is here upon the cross,
> Bound to a road that's dark with blood,
> Guarding immitigable loss.
> Have we the strength to strive alone
> Who can no longer worship Christ?
> Is He a God of wood and stone,
> While those who served him writhe and moan,
> On warfare's altar sacrificed?[15]

In 'Stand-to: Good Friday Morning', a short poem from April 1916, Sassoon portrays a soldier asking Christ to wound him so that he can be invalided home:

> I'd been on duty from two till four.
> I went and stared at the dug-out door.
> Down in the frowst I heard them snore.
> 'Stand to!' Somebody grunted and swore.
>   Dawn was misty; the skies were still;
>   Larks were singing; discordant, shrill;
>   *They* seemed happy; but *I* felt ill.
> Deep in water I splashed my way
> Up the trench to our bogged front line.
> Rain had fallen the whole damned night.

> O Jesus, send me a wound to-day,
> And I'll believe in Your bread and wine,
> And get my bloody old sins washed white![16]

Sassoon himself commented on this poem: 'I haven't shown this to any clergyman. But soldiers say they feel like that sometimes. So the parsons must turn over two pages at once and pray for all poor heretics.' Parsons however might have been even more disturbed by another 1916 poem, 'Christ and the Soldier'. The poet acknowledged its limitations as poetry, and it was published only in 1973. But its final verses bring us to the heart of the matter:

> Machine-guns rattled from below the hill;
> High bullets flicked and whistled through the leaves;
> And smoke came drifting from exploding shells.
> Christ said, 'Believe; and I can cleanse your ill.
> I have not died in vain between two thieves;
> Nor made a fruitless gift of miracles.'
>
> The soldier answered, 'Heal me if you will,
> Maybe there's comfort when a soul believes
> In mercy, and we need it in these hells.
> But be you for both sides? I'm paid to kill
> And if I shoot a man his mother grieves.
> Does that come into what your teaching tells?' . . .
>
> 'Lord Jesus, ain't you got no more to say?'
> Bowed hung that head below the crown of thorns.
> The soldier shifted, and picked up his pack,
> And slung his gun, and stumbled on his way.
> 'O God,' he groaned, 'why ever was I born?'
> The battle boomed, and no reply came back.[17]

Perhaps that silence was the only conceivable answer. It would not, after all, be the first time Christ had remained silent in the face of a difficult question; and the silence, either in the trenches or at Golgotha, where he was asked why he did not save himself and the thieves hanging with him (Luke 23:39), need no more be interpreted as cool indifference than the tortured silence of a man keeping his wife company as she lies dying in a hospital bed. In the end it was precisely Golgotha which served Sassoon as metaphor and reference point in 'Reconciliation', dating from November 1918:

> When you are standing at your hero's grave,
> Or near some homeless village where he died,
> Remember, through your heart's rekindling pride,
> The German soldiers who were loyal and brave.
>
> Men fought like brutes; and hideous things were done;
> And you have nourished hatred harsh and blind.
> But in that Golgotha perhaps you'll find
> The mothers of the men who killed your son.[18]

To move from the evocative and eloquent power of Sassoon's poetry to the verse of Geoffrey Studdert Kennedy is to enter a world at once different and yet palpably the same. Studdert Kennedy was, first and foremost, a priest, not a poet: he appears in scarcely any of the books of, or about, First World War poetry; and he certainly made no claims for literary merit. His background was poorer than Sassoon's, and his formation entirely different: he lived and wrote from within the heart of the Church of England, and even in 1914 that was a world away from most people's lives and interests. Yet he too experienced at first hand the atrocious suffering of those in the trenches; and as 'Woodbine Willie' he became the best known and loved army chaplain of the war. His poems are neither more nor less than immediate articulations of his experience, always without artifice and sometimes without depth. But they make a notable contribution to the prayer of protest.

Like Sassoon, Studdert Kennedy rebelled aganst the blatantly nationalist theology popularized by the bellicose Winnington-Ingram; and his satirical poem 'A Sermon' ends with a plea to God to deliver them from pious cant.[19] Unlike Sassoon, however, Studdert Kennedy never lost his deeply held conviction that Christ was within the suffering, silently uniting it with his own. In some of his poems this does not prevent him from extolling the glory of the cause for which Great Britain was fighting, as in 'The Suffering God':

How can it be that God can reign in glory,
    Calmly content with what His Love has done,
Reading unmoved the piteous shameful story,
    All the vile deeds men do beneath the sun?

Are there no tears in the heart of the Eternal?
    Is there no pain to pierce the soul of God?
Then must He be a fiend of Hell infernal,
    Beating the earth to pieces with His rod.

Or is it just that there is nought behind it,
    Nothing but forces purposeless and blind?
Is the last thing, if mortal man could find it,
    Only a power wandering as the wind?

Father, if He, the Christ, were Thy Revealer,
    Truly the First Begotten of the Lord,
Then must Thou be a Suff'rer and a Healer,
    Pierced to the heart by the sorrow of the sword . . .

Passionately fierce the voice of God is pleading,
    Pleading with men to arm them for the fight;
See how those hands, majestically bleeding,
    Call us to rout the armies of the night.

Not to the work of sordid selfish saving
    Of our own souls to dwell with Him on high,
But to the soldier's splendid selfish braving,
    Eager to fight for Righteousness and die.[20]

Here the now embarrassing jingoism sits uncomfortably with the challenge to an uncaring and omnipotent God. It is mercifully absent from most of his other poems, many of which exhibit a more searching spirituality. In 'High and Lifted Up' he castigates purveyors of a triumphalist religion, and denounces the God of power:

Seated on the throne of power with the sceptre
    in Thine hand,

While a host of eager angels ready for Thy Service stand.
So it was the prophet saw Thee, in his agony of prayer,
While the sound of many waters swelled in music on the air,
Swelled until it burst like thunder in a shout of perfect praise,
'Holy, Holy, Holy Father, Potentate of years and days' . . .
But I stand in woe and wonder; God, my God, I cannot see.
Darkness deep and deeper darkness – all the world is dark to
    me.
Where is power? Where is glory? Where is any victory won?
Where is wisdom? Where is honour? Where the splendour of
    the sun?
God, I hate this splendid vision – all its splendour is a lie.
Splendid fools see splendid folly, splendid mirage born to
    die . . .
Preachers give it me for comfort, and I curse them to their
    face,
Puny, petty-minded priestlings prate to me of power and
    grace . . .
All their speech is drowned in sobbing, and I hear the great
    world groan,
As I see a million mothers sitting weeping all alone . . .
And I hate the God of Power on His hellish heavenly throne,
Looking down on rape and murder, hearing little children
    moan . . .[21]

In 'My Peace I Leave With You' Studdert Kennedy answers
the questions of God's justice and presence with the now
familiar picture of the suffering Christ. Yet somehow both the
answer and the style fail to convince, smacking more of a
candlelit church than a sodden trench:

> For millions come to Golgotha
>   To suffer and to die,
> Forsaken in their hour of need,
>   And asking, Why?
>
> Man's Via Crucis never ends,
>   Earth's Calvaries increase,
> The world is full of spears and nails,
>   But where is Peace?

'Take up Thy Cross and follow Me,
  I am the Way, my son,
Via Crucis, Via Pacis,
  Meet and are one.'[22]

But in 'Missing – Believed Killed', subtitled 'On reading a Mother's Letter', Studdert Kennedy allows his (and the bereaved mother's) anger at God to erupt at last:

'Twere heaven enough to fill my heart
  If only one would stay,
Just one of all the million joys
  God gives to take away.

If I could keep one golden dawn,
  The splendour of one star,
One silver glint of yon bird's wing
  That flashes from afar;

If I could keep the least of things
  That makes me catch my breath
To gasp with wonder at God's world.
  And hold it back from death,

It were enough; but death forbids.
  The sunset flames to fade,
The velvet petals of this rose
  Fall withered – brown – decayed.

She only asked to keep one thing,
  The joy-light in his eyes:
God has not even let her know
  Where his dead body lies.

O Grave, where is thy victory?
  O Death, where is thy sting?
Thy victory is ev'rywhere,
  Thy sting's in ev'rything.[23]

Poems such as this, shorn of the crude chauvinism of 'The Suffering God', compensate for their sentimentality by the directness and power of their protest. In 'The Soul of Doubt'

Studdert Kennedy's faith again triumphs in the end; but this time there is nothing glib about its victory over a persistent and pervasive doubt. In 'Tragedy' he confronts a dilemma that Wilfred Owen also engaged with; and it is instructive to see how each addressed it. The dilemma is the confrontation of suffering and beauty: Kennedy, as might by now be expected, comes down on the side of beauty, though again it is a hard-won battle:

> I know. It is not easy to explain
> Why should there be such agony to bear?
> Why should the whole wide world be full of pain?
> But then, why should her hair
> Be like the sudden sunshine after rain?
>
> Turn cynic if you will. Curse God and die.
> You've ample reason for it. There's enough
> Of bitterness, God knows, to answer why.
> The road of life is rough,
> But then there is the glory of the sky . . .[24]

Owen's response, in 'Strange Meeting', is very different, and will be discussed below. Studdert Kennedy's optimism, here as elsewhere, nevertheless does not prevent him from recognizing the depths of the problem; nor does it diminish the extent to which he articulated the anger and the questions people must constantly have felt. His dialect poems, first entitled 'Rough Rhymes of a Padre', may today appear stilted and patronizing; but some of them struggle with the experiences of everyday life in the war in a way that more polished literary productions sometimes fail to do. In 'The Sorrow of God' Studdert Kennedy portrays an ordinary soldier reflecting on how much easier it was to believe in God in leafy countryside than in the midst of war, and wrestling with God about the related issues of suffering and human freedom;[25] and in 'I Know Not Where They Have Laid Him' he captures graphically the prayer of protest of a bereaved woman seeking her son's grave:

I wouldn't mind if I only knowed
   The spot where they'd laid my lad;
If I could see where they'd buried 'im,
   It wouldn't be arf so bad . . .
Parson 'e says as it makes no odds,
   'Cause the soul o' the lad goes on,
'Is spirit 'as gorn to 'is Gawd, 'e says,
   Wherever 'is body 'as gorn.
But Parson ain't never 'ad no child,
   'E's a man, not a woman, see?
'Ow can 'e know what a woman feels
   And what it can mean to me? . . .
What is the body that they shall wear
   Up there in God's Paradise?
I may be a fool, but that's just it,
   That's just what I wants to know . . .
I reckons as 'ow that Scripture piece
   Were writ by a single man;
They never knows what a body costs,
   And I don't see 'ow they can . . .
But I'd like to know just where it's laid,
   That body my body bore,
And I'd like to know who'll mother 'im
   Out there on that other shore.
Who will be bearin' the mother's part
   And be makin' your body, boy?
Who will be 'avin' the mother's pain,
   And feelin' the mother's joy?
Gawd, is it you? Then bow You down
   And 'ark to a mother's prayer.
Don'u keep it all to yourself, Good Lord,
   But give 'is old mother a share.
Gimme a share of the travail pain
   Of my own son's second birth,
Double the pain if you double the joy
   That a mother feels on earth.
Gimme the sorrow and not the joy,
   If that 'as to be Your will;

Gimme the labour and not the pride,
But make me 'is mother still.[26]

As poetry, 'I Know Not Where They Have Laid Him' is
doubtless difficult to defend: as spirituality it is difficult to
dismiss, and hard to escape the feeling that Studdert Kennedy
here lays bare something of what millions of women must
have experienced in the midst of a man's world and a man's
war. This time he offers no hope, and no resort to trembling
piety clouds its close. The same is true of 'Dead and Buried',
in which Kennedy virulently denounces what he and many
others saw as the statesmen's sick betrayal, in the Treaty of
Versailles, of so much that people had fought for. This time
it is the suffering Christ who does the protesting:

I have borne my cross through Flanders,
    Through the broken heart of France,
I have borne it through the deserts of the East;
    I have wandered, faint and longing,
    Through the human hosts that, thronging,
Swarmed to glut their grinning idols with a feast.

    I was crucified in Cambrai,
    And again outside Bapaume;
I was scourged for miles along the Albert Road,
    I was driven, pierced and bleeding,
    With a million maggots feeding
On the body that I carried as my load . . .

    Yet my heart was still unbroken,
    And my hope was still unquenched,
Till I bore my cross to Paris through the crowd.
    Soldiers pierced me on the Aisne,
    But 'twas by the river Seine
That the statesmen brake my legs and made my shroud.

    There they wrapped my mangled body
    In fine linen of fair words,
With the perfume of a sweetly scented lie,
    And they laid it in the tomb

149

Of the golden-mirrored room,
'Mid the many-fountained Garden of Versailles . . .

For it isn't steel and iron
That men use to kill their God,
But the poison of a smooth and slimy tongue.
Steel and iron tear the body,
But it's oily sham and shoddy
That have trampled down God's *Spirit* in the dung.[27]

Studdert Kennedy did not stop writing when the war ended; and some of his later prose works, most of which were written in a kind of fluent but effective journalese, again address the issues raised by the poems discussed here. In 'The Hardest Part', begun during the war and arising directly out of his wartime experiences, he fiercely attacks the soldier praying for his own safety in the trenches as being un-Christlike and cowardly, and instead praises the hefty sergeant for swearing instead: 'This chap's prayer is much more sinful than the sergeant's swears. There is love in the sergeant's blasphemy. He may not be thinking about God, but he is thinking about his platoon. He may not be a Christian, but at any rate he's not a coward.'[28] He goes on to point out that prayer is often unanswered: 'Even as I pray now I may be blown to bits, as Christ, still praying, suffered on the Cross . . .' So the value of prayer consists in 'the only answer worth having, the power to pass through danger and through death with a spirit still unbroken and a manhood still unstained'. And he continues:

Prayer is the means of communication by which the suffering and triumphant God meets His band of volunteers and pours His spirit into them, and sends them out to fight, to suffer, and to conquer in the end.

Prayer will not turn away the shell from my body; it will not change the flight of the bullet; but it will ensure that neither shell nor bullet can touch me, the real me . . . And in the end, through prayer and the army of those that pray, God will reach down to the roots of war and tear them from the world.[29]

It is perhaps at this point that doubts begin to arise. There is something powerful, indeed heroic, about such a view of prayer; and that is precisely why it ultimately fails to convince. The truth is that many of us do feel like the poor soldier reduced to praying for his own safety; and, from the psalmist onward, have poured out our feelings to God. And, if prayer is to have any value at all, it must surely consist in the opportunity it offers us to express what we feel, not just what (according to certain external ideals) we ought to feel, to a God who shares our experiences even if he is powerless to deliver us from them.

For all that, Studdert Kennedy did repeatedly uncover and articulate the depths of human experience in war; and he never lost his capacity to express something of the sheer unequivocal evil that the 'war to end wars' begat. In 'The Word and the Work', written in 1925, he addressed the heart of the Christian dilemma with a power and honesty unmatched by almost any of his poems:

> 'The light shines in the darkness, and the darkness cannot overcome it.' Can't it? Can't it? you say. It can. Millions live and die in the darkness. There is a glimmer of light in childhood while innocency lives on ignorance; then it flickers, fades, and dies, and men go out into the dark. What is the good of your wretched Christian optimism when you know it is not true? Don't you know that men die in the dark? I do; I do. I cannot explain it.[30]

Later in the same book he wrote: 'Life is a tragedy . . . There is no justice in it . . . Love was murdered on the battlefields of France.' And he began the book with a poignant little story about an old French countrywoman devoted to her two cows:

> Then one day when the village, which up to then had escaped bombardment, was heavily shelled, we came upon her sitting on the roadside near to her two cows which had been literally torn to pieces, wiping her wounded face, and crying through her tears: 'Le bon Dieu, il est mort! Le bon Dieu, il est mort!' There is no sense, no meaning in the

151

world; it is mad, it is a dirty, cruel, muddled mess, that grinds and crushes living things to death. That was how it seemed to her.[31]

It was not, in the end, how it seemed to Geoffrey Studdert Kennedy. But that did not prevent him, in poetry and prose, and in countless vivid sermons and addresses delivered up and down the country in the course of a breathlessly busy life, from grasping the essence of people's doubts and anger and puzzlement and grief and pouring them out to a God whose baffling silence was, for Kennedy, neither the cruel indifference of the despot nor the dumb sterility of the idol but the hidden presence of the crucified. This was a prayer of protest that millions could share; and, if the answer it evoked was sometimes dim and doubtful, its author never stopped believing that it was heard.

Not everyone could share Studdert Kennedy's passionate faith in the ultimate triumph of God and goodness; and not everyone will have felt that the huge questions asked in Isaac Rosenberg's terrible and searching poem 'Dead Man's Dump' could be so certainly answered:

> The wheels lurched over sprawled dead
> But pained them not, though their bones crunched,
> Their shut mouths made no moan.
> They lie there huddled, friend and foeman,
> Man born of man, and born of woman,
> And shells go crying over them
> From night till night and now.
>
> Earth has waited for them,
> All the time of their growth
> Fretting for their decay:
> Now she has them at last!
> In the strength of their strength
> Suspended – stopped and held.
>
> What fierce imaginings their dark souls lit?
> Earth! have they gone into you!

Somewhere they must have gone,
And flung on your hard back
Is their soul's sack
Emptied of God-ancestralled essences.
Who hurled them out? Who hurled?[32]

It was perhaps in the poetry of Wilfred Owen that such
questions were most powerfully articulated. Owen and Kennedy had much in common: both were intuitively religious,
Owen having also thought seriously about ordination; both
were in some respects complex and contradictory figures,
driven by a mass of conflicting motives and desires; and both
began the war in fervent patriotic conviction which did not
survive their experiences at the front line. Owen's 1917 poem
'Anthem for Doomed Youth' sharply expresses the bitterness
of his feelings:

What passing-bells for these who die as cattle?
– Only the monstrous anger of the guns.
   Only the stuttering rifles' rapid rattle
Can patter out their hasty orisons.
No mockeries now for them; no prayers nor bells;
   Nor any voice of mourning save the choirs, –
The shrill, demented choirs of wailing shells;
   And bugles calling for them from sad shires.[33]

The vivid and violent image of the young soldiers' last frantic
prayers grimly articulated by the stutter of fatal gunfire gives
the prayer of protest a new and macabre apparel. In a later
poem, 'The Last Laugh', Owen echoes Studdert Kennedy's
point about the sergeant whose blasphemies are indistinguishable from prayer; indeed Owen makes this point explicitly in
his own comments on the poem:

'Oh! Jesus Christ! I'm hit,' he said; and died.
Whether he vainly cursed or prayed indeed,
   The Bullets chirped – In vain, vain, vain!
   Machine-guns chuckled – Tut-tut! Tut-tut!
   And the Big Gun gaffawed.

Another sighed – 'O Mother, – Mother, – Dad!'
Then smiled at nothing, childlike, being dead.
    And the lofty Shrapnel-cloud
    Leisurely gestured, – Fool!
    And the splinters spat, and tittered.

'My Love!' one moaned. Love-languid seemed his mood,
Till slowly lowered, his whole face kissed the mud.
    And the Bayonets' long teeth grinned;
    Rabbles of Shells hooted and groaned;
    And the Gas hissed.

Owen prefaced this poem: 'There is a point where prayer is indistinguishable from blasphemy. There is also a point where blasphemy is indistinguishable from prayer.'[34] In its extremest forms, as Bunyan pointed out, the prayer of protest is not an eloquent patterned oration, nor even the selfless prayer for God's will to be done that Studdert Kennedy extolled: it was no more or less than a scream or a word. And for Wilfred Owen, as for so many others, it was met by silence. Even nature was cold and unresponsive; and this returns us to the conflict, described by Studdert Kennedy in 'Tragedy', between beauty and tragedy. We have already seen that, for Kennedy, beauty was ultimately triumphant – or at least that its power provided a strong enough challenge to tragedy to enable faith and hope to endure. One might have expected Owen, whose earlier poems reflect much of the earlier Romantic poets' evocation of the transcendental power of beauty, to have agreed. But by 1917 he could not; and his poem 'Exposure', with its devastating contrasts between agony and death on the one hand and 'blossoms trickling where the blackbird fusses' on the other, hammers home his despair: even 'love of God seems dying'.[35]

Nowhere is this rendered more savagely explicit than in the poem that many have perceived to be Owen's greatest, 'Strange Meeting'. The title and theme come from Shelley, and the poem was eloquently set to music in the closing section of Benjamin Britten's *War Requiem*; but the immense power of the writing is Owen's alone. The grim and graphic vision of hell, where the soldier encounters one he has killed, leads to a reflection by the dead enemy on what is inescapably the heart of the matter:

> 'Strange friend,' I said, 'here is no cause to mourn.'
> 'None,' said that other, 'save the undone years,
> The hopelessness. Whatever hope is yours,
> Was my life also; I went hunting wild
> After the wildest beauty in the world,
> Which lies not calm in eyes, or braided hair,
> But mocks the steady running of the hour,
> And if it grieves, grieves richlier than here.'

The love of beauty which alone had defied the power of death because it gave people a vision of ultimate truth was itself reduced to mourning, 'richlier than here' – mourning, that is, more intensely in the world of the trenches than in the cold grey half-world of death. And the enemy soldier continues:

> For by my glee might many men have laughed,
> And of my weeping something had been left,
> Which must die now. I mean the truth untold,
> The pity of war, the pity war distilled.
> Now men will go content with what we spoiled,
> Or, discontent, boil bloody, and be spilled.
> They will be swift with swiftness of the tigress.
> None will break ranks, though nations trek from
>   progress.

The deep pessimism of these lines, the dying of truth itself, the loss even of the compassion that war itself created, and the terrible prophetic power of Owen's description of the nations trekking away from progress – in a world where so recently 'trek' and 'progress' had come to symbolize all that was most hopeful and heroic in civilization – reach their climax in the poem's bleak and spare ending:

> 'I am the enemy you killed, my friend,
> I knew you in this dark: for so you frowned

Yesterday through me as you jabbed and killed.
I parried; but my hands were loath and cold.
Let us sleep now . . .'[36]

Despite the rapt beauty of Britten's setting of these lines in
the *War Requiem*, this is not the peace of eternal rest so much
as the hopeless shroud of death; not Easter but Golgotha. In
its almost unbearably moving imagery and pathos, 'Strange
Meeting' is reminiscent of the terrible eighty-eighth psalm
that was discussed in Chapter 3. In one sense, of course,
Owen's poem is not prayer at all: in another it becomes
inescapably the raw material of all prayer thereafter. For its
deep despair, its unequivocal acknowledgement that truth
and beauty and compassion all died on the Western Front,
offer the spirituality of protest the only conceivable way forward: a frank acceptance that *this* is the way things are, and
that prayer will now be offered in a world where blind tragedy
has triumphed over beauty, and the voice of God is silent.

Yet the poem was written. Like Psalm 88, or the verses of
Sassoon and Studdert Kennedy and many others, the hope
lies only in the very articulation of hopelessness. Studdert
Kennedy was, in this at least, right enough: centuries earlier
someone else had died young and unfulfilled with a cry of
despair on his lips; and perhaps he did indeed die again
among millions of others between 1914 and 1918. Perhaps,
for him and for them, a way forward is to be found only once
the full extent of what is happening has been confronted and
expressed, so that the prayer of protest becomes a small but
vital part of that process of facing the reality of the present
without which there can be no future worth expecting, and
no hope that is worth the name. If that is so, then the poets of
the First World War will have done the world an inestimable
service. But the land of lost content could never be the same
again:

> Into my heart an air that kills
> From yon far country blows:
> What are those blue remembered hills,
> What spires, what farms are those?

156

That is the land of lost content,
I see it shining plain,
The happy highways where I went
And cannot come again.[37]

NOTES

1   quoted in *The Time of Our Lives: growing up in the Southwark area 1900–1945* (London, Peckham Publishing Project, 1983), p. 52.
2   *Strange Meeting* (London, Penguin, 1974), p. 155.
3   quoted in Alan Wilkinson, *The Church of England and the First World War* (London, SPCK, 1978), p. 253.
4   quoted in Lyn Macdonald, *They Called it Passchendaele* (London, Macmillan, 1978), p. 168.
5   'February Afternoon' from *Collected Poems*. (London, Faber, 1936.)
6   quoted in Jon Silkin, *Out of Battle: the poetry of the Great War* (London, Ark Paperbacks, 1987), p. 140. See also the powerful reflection on the same theme in Henri Barbusse's novel *Le feu*, published in England as *Under Fire*; quoted in Wilkinson, op. cit. p. 109.
7   'Carol', quoted in Martin Stephen, *Never Such Innocence: a new anthology of Great War verse* (London, Buchan & Enright, 1988), p. 117.
8   Untitled poem, quoted in ibid. pp. 115–16.
9   Tr. from the Russian by David McDuff and Jon Silkin in *The Penguin Book of First World War Poetry*, ed. Jon Silkin, 2nd edn (London, Penguin, 1981), p. 266.
10   quoted in Wilkinson, op. cit. pp. 236–7.
11   quoted in ibid. p. 113.
12   quoted in ibid. p. 133.
13   Sassoon, *The War Poems* (London, Faber, 1983), p. 57. For 'Vicarious Christ' see ibid. p. 141.
14   'Now, God be thanked Who has matched us with His hour . . .' from 'Peace', in *Rupert Brooke: the poetical works*, ed. Keynes (London, Faber, 1970), p. 19.
15   Sassoon, op. cit. p. 19.
16   ibid. p. 28.
17   ibid. p. 46.
18   ibid. p. 136.

19 Studdert Kennedy, *The Unutterable Beauty* (Oxford, Mowbrays, 1983), pp. 32–5.
20 ibid. pp. 12–13.
21 ibid. pp. 40–1.
22 ibid. p. 77.
23 ibid. p. 80.
24 ibid. p. 95.
25 ibid. pp. 115–20. See also William Purcell, *Woodbine Willie: a study of Geoffrey Studdert Kennedy* (Oxford, Mowbrays, 1962), p. 131.
26 Studdert Kennedy, op. cit. pp. 147–9.
27 ibid. pp. 69–71. See also Purcell, op. cit. pp. 152–3.
28 'The Hardest Part', quoted in *The Best of Studdert Kennedy* (London, Hodder & Stoughton, 1947), p. 49.
29 ibid. pp. 53–4.
30 *The Word and the Work* (London, Longmans, 1925), pp. 37, 55.
31 ibid. pp. 3–4.
32 Rosenberg, 'Dead Man's Dump', in *The Penguin Book of First World Poetry*, op. cit. p. 211.
33 *The Poems of Wilfred Owen*, ed. Stallworthy (London, Hogarth, 1985), p. 76.
34 ibid. p. 145.
35 ibid. pp. 162–3.
36 ibid. pp. 125–6.
37 A. E. Housman, 'A Shropshire Lad', 40.

FURTHER READING

Siegfried Sassoon, *The War Poems*, arr. Rupert Hart-Davis. London, Faber, 1983.

G. A. Studdert Kennedy, *The Unutterable Beauty*. Oxford, Mowbrays, 1983.

The Poems of Wilfred Owen, ed. Jon Stallworthy. London, Hogarth, 1985.

Jon Silkin, *Out of Battle: the poetry of the Great War*. London, Routledge & Kegan Paul, Ark Paperbacks, 1987.

The Penguin Book of First World War Poetry, ed. Jon Silkin, 2nd edn. Penguin, 1981.

William Purcell, *Woodbine Willie: a study of Geoffrey Studdert Kennedy*. Oxford, Mowbrays, 1962, repr. 1983.

Jon Stallworthy, *Wilfred Owen: a biography*. Oxford University Press, 1977.

Martin Stephen, *Never Such Innocence: a new anthology of Great War verse*. London, Buchan & Enright, 1988.

Alan Wilkinson, *The Church of England and the First World War*. London, SPCK, 1978.

Lyn Macdonald, *They Called It Passchendaele*. London, Macmillan, 1983.

John Lehmann, *The English Poets of the First World War*. London, Thames & Hudson, 1982.

Paul Fussell, *The Great War and Modern Memory*. Oxford University Press, 1975.

Susan Hill, *Strange Meeting*. London, Penguin, 1974.

10

The Songs of Freedom
The Holocaust and Beyond

Two key themes have emerged from our exploration of the prayer of protest; and it may help to summarize both and consider their implications before concluding by exploring two contemporary aspects of this kind of prayer.

The first theme that we have sought to explore is the relationship of protest and love. The prayer of protest, from its biblical sources onwards, constantly underlines the importance of seeing spirituality in the context of a mutual relationship strong enough to absorb challenge and doubt as well as affection and trust, and broad enough to embrace every aspect of human experience. The crucial point is to see that these apparently diverse ingredients in fact belong together: it is, as we have seen, *because* Israel has in some sense experienced God's love that she felt able to cry out and protest when she experienced God's anger, or (perhaps worse) God's silence. We may not (indeed we almost certainly will not) share a view of providence that holds disaster or suffering to be directly God's will, let alone to be the direct result of our wickedness. But that need not stop us learning from what underlies such a view: the searching realism that refuses to take refuge in the two most persistently endemic adversaries of true spirituality, idealization and fantasy; the stubborn insistence that adversity of every kind (and life itself) is to be struggled with and made sense of in the light of the idea or reality of God.

Such a spirituality will be costly however, and for at least three reasons. First any genuine encounter with God, as with another human being – any situation in which we are unconditionally open to another person – is a hazardous affair.

160

Perhaps one of the reasons why we so often find prayer tedious is that we are distinctly reluctant to allow ourselves or our views to be changed by engaging in it. It need not matter that, as J. C. Squire pointed out (see Chapter 9), people on different sides in the world's conflicts pour out to God prayers whose aspirations directly contradict each other; but it matters very much if such prayer is designed only to harden our convictions rather than to dispose us for an encounter with God which might even cause us to change them. There is something depressing, and almost chillingly amusing, about the spectacle of Christians holding sharply different views on contentious issues, and then piously praying for God's will to be done – always provided, of course, that it does not happen to conflict with theirs. If any genuine and mutual relationship needs to find space for challenge and protest, it can do so only by first presupposing the possibility of honest and courageous changes of mind, and secondly fostering that clarity of thought and freedom from illusory fears or fantasies that alone make such changes possible.

In turn this leads us to the second reason why such prayer will be costly. If we are to take seriously the context of prayer as a two-way relationship, then we also need to take seriously the possibility of God protesting to us. This is a formidably difficult area: there has never been a shortage of people claiming direct lines to the Creator, and history is littered with the dire consequences of such people's insistence that they alone act in his name. Yet that in itself may be a compelling reason for learning to listen more sensitively; and if the prayer of protest helps us all humbly to discern God's sorrowing anger at the wanton destruction of both creation and creatures, it may lead not to arrogant posturing but to genuine and urgent action for change. If we are to have the courage to tell God, in effect, what we think of him and his world, we should not be surprised if from time to time he does the same to us. And the marks of his protest and sorrow, now as in the time of Jeremiah, will be innocent and unmerited suffering – suffering that is the direct consequence of others' greed or silence. It is in that sense that some of the Psalms can be understood both as the cry of the despairing and as God's own prayer;

or the *Benedicite* as the divine protest against the rape of the earth, the blind extermination of animal species and rain forest against the spectral background of nuclear confrontation. In a powerful conclusion to a book that deserves to be much better known, the Scottish writer Ian M. Fraser suggests the creative possibilities inherent in a spirituality where our protest and God's collide:

> The fruit of our struggle with God may well be to discover the coincidence between his purposes and the fulfilment of our own personal beings and of our societies . . . The fruit of Jacob's wrestling was a new and enhanced identity and place in God's purpose. Once Moses took the road to deliver his people he found that he was equipped as he went and was able effectively to do what he had effectively argued was impossible. Jesus disputed the will of the Father, holding himself open to the possibility that that will held the true meaning of his life: so he was led to take a sure, sacrificial road to salvation for humanity. The kingdom is to be taken by storm. Those who fight God to the last ditch may wrest from him what he has in store for them as a gift. Only if we are prepared to unmask God and find his name is it possible to discover our own.[1]

Thirdly, however, such prayer will be costly because the love it presupposes is costly too. The poetry of the Song of Songs, the spirituality of St Teresa, John Bunyan and the people of the desert tradition, all testify to the nature of intimate love as letting go, even as death. It is worth instancing a modern example of what this may mean. In his book *The Hard Awakening* H. B. Dehqani-Tafti, the Anglican Bishop in Iran, describes what happened to him and his people following the revolution of 1978–9: the church's property was sequestrated, he was forced into exile and his son Bahraam was murdered. The Bishop's response to this is both instructive and deeply moving. He cries out in a prayer that precisely exemplifies the subject of this book: 'O God, we as a family are going through Good Friday. When will the Resurrection be? When will Bahraam's sacrifice give fruit?'[2] He later points out that there is no room in Christianity for the Shiite doctrine of *taqieyh*, or tactical dissimulation, hiding your feelings for the sake of some short-term advantage; and he certainly does not attempt to hide his.[3] Yet in turn this leads him to allow his love and anger and bitterness to be turned to good account, helping him and others like him to move beyond the articulation of their feelings to a deeper concern to bring something creative out of what has happened, so that Bahraam's tragic sacrifice may indeed become redemptive.

This brings us to our second major theme. It was argued at the outset that the prayer of protest comprised both challenge and questioning, and the honest laying bare of our own experience: protest, that is, both in the sense of dissent and in the sense of bearing witness. The writers we have studied may have helped us to see why this matters so much: partly because, like Job, we cannot move on beyond suffering until we have first wrestled with it or come to terms with it; partly because, like Julian of Norwich, the very act of protest will demand of us a rigorous and unflinching contemplation of reality without which all spirituality is no more than hot air; partly because, like the adherents of apocalyptic, we may thereby discover a hope that can sustain us even while we are immured in doubt or darkness; and partly too because such twofold protest presupposes some kind of faith in *yourself*, an implicit conviction that *your* experience counts and has value. This last point is crucial: it is not to imply that all our praying must be limited by our own experience – indeed we saw in Chapter 2 the enormous value of the imagination in helping us to transcend that experience. But it is to imply that it must begin there. When so much of modern life tends to diminish the human person, reducing human beings to statistics or passive consumers, and inducing in us a helpless apathy in the face of bureaucracy and vast structures of institutional control, we urgently need a spirituality that gently and critically affirms the divinely given value of each of us, the holiness of each person's life, the sacramental power in each person's raw and kaleidoscopic experience. When we begin to see this, we may find that the prayer of protest leads to the prayer of contemplative love; for by learning to become,

as it were, more present to ourselves, we may discover a
deeper and more immediate sense of what it means to be
present to others, and to God.

There is space here to instance only two illustrations of
what this means for contemporary life, the first characteristic
of human experience in all ages, the second a distinctive
aspect of the twentieth century. Bishop Dehqani-Tafti's
reflections have already touched on one of the most universal
and painful dimensions of human life: the experience of loss
or bereavement. It is important to remember, even in the
brief exploration that follows, that such loss can take many
forms: loss of status or employment, or health or youth, are
often as difficult to cope with as loss of a partner or child. In
her study of this subject Dorothée Soelle suggests that there
are three phases in our response to the experience of suffering
in general, and of loss in particular: the first is apathy, characterized by silence and isolation. The second is articulation,
characterized by lament, expression and (as she puts it)
'psalmic language'. The third is action, characterized by
change and a deeper sense of solidarity with others. She
observes that liturgy in the sense of corporate prayer and
worship can help people through the second phase so as to
lead them on to the third. And she writes, 'I consider the
stage of lament, of articulation, the stage of psalms, to be an
indispensable step on the way to the third stage, in which
liberation and help for the unfortunate can be organized.'[4]

Much work has been done on the importance of this
'lament' phase in the overall process of coming to terms with
bereavement, and not all of it in modern times. In one of his
sermons on the Song of Songs, St Bernard of Clairvaux
mourns the loss of his brother Gerard. He challenges those
who tell him not to weep:

> I am that unhappy portion prostrate in the mud, mutilated
> by the loss of its nobler part, and shall people say to me:
> 'Do not weep'? My very heart is torn from me and shall it
> be said to me: 'Try not to feel it'? But I do feel it . . .[5]

And he acutely touches on the heart of his sense of loss:

I grieve for you, my dearest Gerard, not for the sake of grieving, but because you have been separated from me. Perhaps my grieving should be on my own account, because the cup I drink is bitter. And I grieve by myself because I drink by myself: for you cannot join me. All by myself I experience the sufferings that are shared equally by lovers when compelled to remain apart.[6]

Other writers on the same subject direct these sentiments more explicitly at God. In *A Grief Observed* C. S. Lewis, while recalling Christ's cry of pain at Golgotha, wonders whether that makes his own bereavement after his wife's painful death any easier to understand; and later he passionately asks God why he took such trouble to 'force this creature out of its shell' only to allow it to die horribly from cancer.[7] There is an intensely moving point in Susan Hill's novel *In the Springtime of the Year* when Ruth, whose husband has been tragically killed by a falling tree, comes across the curate Ratheman in the woods, praying in protest at the death of his daughter:

'My daughter is dead.'
And then he struggled to his feet and stood and shouted out, so that the whole wood rang with it, he raved like a man demented.
'She is dead, and where are you now, God, where is all your love and goodness, when she was in pain and there was nothing to ease it, and now she is dead, and what do you know of it, what do you care? What have I got left? Why didn't you kill me, why not me? Wouldn't I have been glad of it? But my child is dead and I . . .'
The shouting faltered and ceased. He looked up, through the canopy of fading leaves, to the patches of sky. Ruth thought, something will happen to him, he will be struck down. A tree will fall. The sky will fall. And she felt a moment of pure terror, fear for the man and fear of him. Nothing happened. The rain fell. And Ratheman began to weep again, covering his face with his hands.
'God forgive me,' he said, 'Oh, God forgive me.'[8]

Finally Dorothée Soelle herself describes her experience after her divorce:

> Everything I had built and hoped for, believed and wanted, had been dashed to pieces. It was as though one who was very, very dear to me had been taken away by death. But the loss and separation occasioned by a marriage gone on the rocks necessarily involves the matter of guilt. One cannot escape the sense of guilt, of having forgotten or failed to do something, of having made a dreadful mistake that could not be soothed and calmed by some kind of belief in fate. It took me three years to overcome and come to terms with the suicidal thoughts and desires that filled my mind. It seems as though the only hope and desire I had was to die. It was in this state of mind that while on a trip to Belgium I visited a late-Gothic-style church. I realize now that 'prayer' is not the right term. I was crying out. I was crying out for help, and the only kind of help I could conceive of or want was that my husband would come back to me.[9]

In all such cases the prayer of protest, the 'lament' phase, offers more than simply a way of off-loading your anger and bitterness on to God's convenient shoulders. It also offers a means of coming to terms with the whole of what is happening to you, capturing in your prayer both the intensity of what you loved and have lost, and the extremity of your suffering in losing it. To be able to do that, either alone or in a shared act of liturgy, is an indispensable part of the search for resolution and a way forward.

The second area in which the implications of this aspect of the prayer of protest can be illustrated is no less than the context in which we now live. I was born at the end of a decade which, together with its predecessor, witnessed what were probably the two most appalling acts of unrestricted and unmitigated evil that the world has ever known. This is not a book about the Holocaust, or the purges of Stalin, partly because so much has already been written about them by people much better qualified than I am to reflect upon them, and partly because I did not live through them. But I do live *after* them; and any book which is at all concerned with the problem of reconciling God with undeserved suffering must recognize that they happened, and acknowledge their shadow. The words of Abraham Lewin, whose diary of the Warsaw ghetto stands as one of the great testimonies to the enduring importance of articulating our experience, even in the midst of a tragedy that still stands in judgment on us all, may represent the prayer of millions whose lives were savagely cut short in our own century:

> Those who are far away cannot imagine our bitter situation. They will not understand and will not believe that day after day thousands of men, women and children, innocent of any crime, were taken to their death. And the handful of those remaining after nine weeks is in mortal danger and, it seems, can expect the same fate. Almighty God! Why did this happen? And why is the whole world deaf to our screams?[10]

The Holocaust matters because it destroyed at a stroke any remaining illusions humanity could conceivably have cherished about a God who effortlessly dispenses good and evil as reward or punishment for human conduct. It also dramatically and drastically alters both the perspective of our lives and the contours of our spirituality: if six million men, women and children could be massacred while the rest of the world went about its business, what other appalling horrors is humanity capable of committing? A spirituality that does not even begin to acknowledge the huge questions and the radically urgent perspective that such events summon us to address is not any longer a spirituality worthy of the name. Elie Wiesel, who alone of his family survived imprisonment in Auschwitz, described in *Night* the flames that murdered God as well as countless adults and children, and that consumed his faith for ever.[11] Yet there is a sense in which he could not let God go, perhaps (as one author suggested) 'because that act may be one way to testify that the human heart was not completely incinerated at Auschwitz'.[12]

167

Elsewhere in his work Wiesel himself offers hints of explanation. In *A Jew Today* he describes the one remaining member of a Jewish family saying to God:

> Master of the Universe, I know what you want – I understand what You are doing. You want despair to overwhelm me. You want me to cease believing in You, to cease praying to You, to cease invoking Your name to glorify and sanctify it. Well, I tell you: No, no – a thousand times no! You shall not succeed! In spite of me and in spite of You, I shall shout the Kaddish, which is a song of faith, for You and against You. This song You shall not still, God of Israel.[13]

We pray to God because he has too much to answer for to be allowed simply to disappear, because we have to protest *against* him as well as *to* him, and because the only alternative is despair, or silence. In *The Testament* Elie Wiesel expresses this perhaps better than anyone else has done:

> Only, in my imagination, the dead are not mute; they speak, they cry out. The massacred Jews of Barassy and Liyanov, the fighters struck down in Spain, the men and women of so many forgotten or burned cemeteries, they pray, they sing, they lament: how is one to silence them? . . . And I understood why God created heaven and earth, why He fashioned man in His image by conferring on him the right and the ability to speak his joy, to express his anguish.
> God too, God himself, was afraid of silence.[14]

From the inarticulate cries of animals or children deprived of their mothers, to the moving laments of the bereaved or the passionate anger of the unjustly oppressed, the prayer of protest is our first (and sometimes our only possible) response to what happens to us. The conviction that underlies this book is that such prayer is made in company with the millions who have so prayed before us and will so pray after us; that it is never prayed alone; and that it is never prayed unheard. A final quotation from Wiesel points its ultimate purpose:

> One of the Just Men came to Sodom, determined to save its inhabitants from sin and punishment. Night and day he walked the streets and markets protesting against greed and theft, falsehood and indifference. In the beginning, people listened and smiled ironically. Then they stopped listening: he no longer even amused them. The killers went on killing, the wise kept silent, as if there were no Just Man in their midst.
>
> One day a child, moved by compassion for the unfortunate teacher, approached him with these words:
>
> 'Poor stranger, you shout, you scream, don't you see that it is hopeless?'
>
> 'Yes, I see,' answered the Just Man.
>
> 'Then why do you go on?'
>
> 'I'll tell you why. In the beginning, I thought I could change man. Today, I know I cannot. If I still shout today, if I still scream, it is to prevent man from ultimately changing me.'[15]

We pray in protest in the hope that we may, to some minute degree, change the world. But even if we do not, we may at least find that our halting efforts to express before God how we feel, and what we (or others) have experienced, may save us from despair.

In the end, however, the prayer of protest is something more than a kind of insurance cover against despair. From Moses to Elie Wiesel it has served to remind us that the search for God and for meaning and wholeness in our lives begins by struggling to make some sense of what we experience; that fate is not simply to be passively accepted but actively engaged with and contested; and that there is room, in our relationship with God, however fragile or tenuous that might be, for vigorous challenge as well as humility and love – indeed that the more we pursue the one, the more we may discover the other too. It reminds us that prayer is something accessible to everyone, requiring no skill or qualifications, even though (like any other branch of human activity) it is likely to improve with practice. It reminds us too that prayer must always find a place for the spontaneous, the charismatic, the prophetic, the unpredictable, even if on occasions it verges close to the inarticulate or even (as Wilfred Owen pointed out) to the blasphemous.[16] It offers us a way of praying that may help us develop a new and urgent perspective in a dangerous world, stripping away our illusory security, jolting our flaccid and complacent sense that such things can never happen to us, or that what happens to AIDS victims or in debates on nuclear power are not our concern. Finally and most important of all, it reminds us that such things – in fact all things – are not only our concern, but God's too; and our prayer of protest may not only enlarge our capacity to address them. It may also enlarge his.

How do we make such prayer our own? Some suggestions have been made in the biblical chapters about possible applications of what has been explored. No aspect of spirituality is more personal than this; and we must learn to pray our own prayers, not simply conform to those printed in books or handed to us by other people. Yet spirituality is never *exclusively* personal; and our own prayer is likely to be immeasurably enriched if it is regularly shared with that of others. Indeed one might go further: in a church faced with massive questions about its identity and purpose, with an ordained ministry severely reduced in size, and with daunting challenges of evangelism and even of maintenance in both urban and rural areas, it may be that the prayer of protest has something to offer on a corporate as well as an individual level. In developing an appropriate strategy for the future the Church will need to assist in the establishing of small groups of Christians, meeting regularly together in each other's homes or workplaces, and by reflecting rigorously both on their own experiences and on the biblical texts, to allow each to collide with the other. Such cells of prayer, united regularly to each other in eucharistic fellowship, and witnessing like the desert people to the living presence of God in the heart of city and countryside, could still provide sources of renewal,

companionship and persistent hope, and in many places
already do. They will need to be linked in acts of worship
that do not balk from articulating the prayer of protest:
funeral rites willing to allow feelings of hope, thanksgiving
and anger to be mingled and offered; and communal liturgy
which allows space for the whole of human experience to
collide with the enduring promise of Christ's gospel. It is all
too rare for Christian worship to embody the depth and power
of this Jewish liturgy in remembrance of the Holocaust:

Reader	Whether the Messiah comes, Ani maamin. Or is late in coming, Ani maamin. Whether God is silent Or weeps, Ani maamin.
Congregation	Ani maamin for him, In spite of him. I believe in You, Even against Your will. Even if you punish me For believing in You.
Reader	Blessed are the fools Who shout their faith. Blessed are the fools Who go on laughing, Who mocks the man who mocks the Jew, Who help their brothers Singing over and over and over:
Congregation	Ani Maamin, ani maamin beviat ha- Mashiah . . .[17]

The primary text of such communities, their basic point of
reference, is likely to be the psalter. From monastic communities to Penetecostal prayer fellowships, from individual priests
and ministers unlocking doors and lighting candles before
reciting the daily office in freezing Victorian churches to tiny

cells of lay Christians gathering round firesides on February nights, and from Jews in ghettos or gulags to Christ at Calvary, the psalter remains the indispensable coping-stone of the prayer of protest; and if I had not found it to be so, this book would never even have been started. It is true that the theology of the Psalms is sometimes unacceptable, and the sentiments sometimes outrageous; and there are in any case some excellent and powerful adaptations written to suit contemporary situations by such people as Ernesto Cardenal in Nicaragua and Zephania Kameeta in Namibia.[18] Yet over and over again, in good times and at crisis points, at great festivals or on cold grey Monday mornings, I have found myself thinking as I read a psalm: that is *exactly* how I feel; that must be just what that person I saw in hospital, or those survivors of a recent earthquake, will be going through. For Christians texts like the 116th Psalm, which Jesus is likely to have recited immediately before entering Gethsemane (cf. Matt. 26:30), will vividly evoke the prayer, the passion and the resurrection of Christ; and for millions, Jews, Christians and others alike, these inspired poems are songs of freedom sung in the heart of slavery, embodying precisely that hope-in-the-midst-of-despair which writers of apocalyptic and victims of injustice everywhere celebrate. On hearing from friends in Germany in 1938 of the terrible events of the Kristallnacht, when synagogues and Jewish property throughout the country were viciously ransacked and Jews themselves rounded up or killed, Dietrich Bonhoeffer counselled Christians and Jews alike to offer the 74th Psalm for and with all those who suffered. In its exact and untrammelled grasp both of the essence of protest and of the indestructibility of hope, and in its capacity to articulate the experience of millions yesterday, today and doubtless tomorrow, this psalm is prayer and sacrament, for our own journeys and beyond:

O God, why have you utterly cast us off?
why is your wrath so hot against the sheep of your pasture?
Turn your steps toward the endless ruins;
the enemy has laid waste everything in your sanctuary.

They said to themselves, 'Let us destroy them altogether.'
They burned down all the meeting-places of God in the
    land.
There are no signs for us to see;
there is no prophet left;
there is not one among us who knows how long.
How long, O God, will the adversary scoff?
will the enemy blaspheme your Name for ever?
Yet God is my King from ancient times,
victorious in the midst of the earth.
Look upon your covenant;
the dark places of the earth are haunts of violence.
Let not the oppressed turn away ashamed;
let the poor and needy praise your name.[19]

NOTES

1   Ian M. Fraser, *The Fire Runs* (London, SCM, 1975), pp. 138–9.
2   H. B. Dehqani-Tafti, *The Hard Awakening* (London, SPCK Triangle, 1981), p. 81.
3   ibid. p. 103.
4   *Suffering*, tr. Kalin (London, DLT, 1975), p. 74.
5   Bernard of Clairvaux, *On the Song of Songs*, vol. II, tr. Walsh, Cistercian Fathers series no. 7 (London, Mowbrays, 1976), p. 68.
6   ibid. p. 70.
7   C. S. Lewis, *A Grief Observed* (London, Faber, 1961), pp. 9, 18.
8   Susan Hill, *In the Springtime of the Year* (London, Penguin, 1977), p. 143.
9   Dorothée Soelle, *The Inward Road*, tr. Scheidt (London, DLT, 1979), pp. 31–2.
10   Abraham Lewin, *A Cup of Tears: a diary of the Warsaw Ghetto*, ed. Polonsky (Oxford, Blackwell, 1988), p. 183.
11   Wiesel, *Night*, tr. Rodway (London, Penguin, 1981), p. 45.
12   R. L. Rubenstein and J. K. Roth, *Approaches to Auschwitz: the legacy of the Holocaust* (London, SCM, 1987), p. 285.
13   Wiesel, *A Jew Today*, quoted in Rubenstein and Roth, op. cit. p. 287.
14   Wiesel, *The Testament*, tr. M. Wiesel (London, Penguin Books, 1982), p. 181.

15 Wiesel, *One Generation After*,. quoted in *The Testament*, op. cit. p. 7.
16 There is an important study of this aspect of prayer, which in turn sheds much light on the prayer of protest as a whole, in Friedrich Heiler's seminal work *Prayer: history and psychology*, tr. McComb (New York, Oxford University Press, Galaxy Books, 1958), ch. IX.
17 'A liturgical offering for Yom Ha-Shoah' in Elie Wiesel and Albert Friedlander, *The Six Days of Destruction: meditations towards hope* (Oxford, Pergamon, 1988), p. 69.
18 Ernesto Cardenal, *Psalms* (London, Search Press); Zephania Kameeta, *Why, O Lord?: psalms and sermons from Namibia* (Geneva, Risk Books, no. 28, 1986).
19 Psalm 74 (New York, Seabury Press, 1977).

Index

Advent 71
Antony of Egypt, St 82–4
apocalyptic 62–78
Aristotle 27
Athanasius, St 82
Augustine of Hippo, St 35–6, 79

Barth, Karl 28
Benedicite 63, 68, 74, 162
bereavement, prayer
   and 164–6
Bernard of Clairvaux,
   St 36–7, 108, 164
Boesak, Allan 73–4, 77
Bonhoeffer, Dietrich 172
Book of Common
   Prayer 118–19, 127
Britten, Benjamin 155–6
Brooke, Rupert 141
Bunyan, John 118–34

Capellanus, Andreas 29
Cardenal, Ernesto 172
Carretto, Carlo 86
Cassian, John 44–5, 87
contemplation, prayer
   of 91–100
Covenanters, Scottish 121–2
Creighton, Oswin 139

Daniel, Book of 62–4, 67, 70

Dehqani-Tafti, H. B. 162, 164
Delp, Alfred 72–3, 77
Desert Fathers 81–9
Dies Irae 76–7

Elijah 80–1, 87

Foucauld, Charles de 79, 82, 84–9

Gandhi, Mahatma 6
Gibbon, Edward 81–2, 85

Hill, Susan 136, 165
Holocaust, prayer and
   the 166–72
Hosea, Book of 88
Housman, A. E. 135

image, language of 33–4

Jeremiah 18–22
Jerome, St 46
Jesus, and prayer as
   protest 22–5, 172
Job, Book of 42–61, 163
John of the Cross, St 108–10, 122
Julian of Norwich 91–101, 163

Kameeta, Zephania 172

175

King, Martin Luther   4
Knox, Ronald   27

Lewin, Abraham   167
Lewis, C. S.   39, 165
Little Brothers and Sisters of
  Jesus   85–6

Mendelssohn, Felix   47
Merton, Thomas   68, 79
Moses   14–17, 80, 88

Nunc Dimittis   70–1, 73

Owen, Wilfred   147, 153–6,
  170

Paul, St   27, 113
Psalms, Book of   24, 42–61,
  126, 128, 161, 171–3

Revelation, Book of   66–7, 71,
  73, 76–7
Rosenberg, Isaac   152

Saki (H. H. Munro)   138
Sassoon, Siegfried   140–3
Shostakovich, Dmitri   48
Singer, Isaac Bashevis   48
Soelle, Dorothée   10, 23, 164,
  166
Song of Songs   26–41
Squire, J. C.   138, 161
Studdert Kennedy,
  Geoffrey   143–54, 156

Te Deum laudamus   74
Teresa of Avila, St   102–17
Thomas, Edward   138
time, prayer and   66–9
Tsvetayeva, Marina   139

Voillaume, René   85–6

waiting, prayer and   69–73
Wiesel, Elie   6, 167–9
Winnington-Ingram, A.
  F.   137, 140